CHEF Q IN Paris
THE WINTER COLLECTION

DIDIER QUEMENER

velvet morning press

Published by Velvet Morning Press

Copyright © 2016 by Didier Quémener

All rights reserved. No part of this book may be reproduced or transmitted in any form or by any means, electronic or mechanical, including photocopying, recording, or by any information storage and retrieval system, without permission in writing from the author, except for the inclusion of brief quotations in a review.

ISBN-13: 978-0997767629
ISBN-10: 0997767626

Cover Design: Ellen Meyer and Vicki Lesage
Author Photo: The Michel Roux Jr Cookery School, Cactus Kitchens
Photo Credit: Didier Quémener and Marie Piantoni

To Phèdre, who tested all of the chocolate recipes.

To A. Craig Copetas for being such a good friend: I'll make sure you eat your share of veggies this winter!

To my grandfather, who taught me not only to respect nature, but also to properly work with it, and shared his knowledge of seasonal products with me every day.

Table of Contents

Introduction 1
Soups 5
    Odette's French Onion Soup 6
    Potato & Bacon Soup 10
    The Ultimate Chicken Soup 14
    Cream of Parsnip 18
Main Courses 23
    Turkey Breast with Normandy Cream Sauce 24
    Purée of Winter Veggies with a Twist 28
    Beer Lamb Stew 34
    Linguine with Butternut Squash 38
Desserts & Drinks 43
    Intense Chocolate Cake 44
    Poached Pears in Red Wine and Spices 48
    Chocolate-*Pralin* Mini Bread Puddings 52
    Chocolate *Café Crème* 56
    Traditional Hot Chocolate 60
Which Tea for Your Macarons? 64
The Perfect Valentine's Day Dinner 66
    Royal Passion 66
    Apple Cheese Puff 67
    Roasted Hake with Potatoes & Sautéed Cherry Tomatoes ... 68
    Champagne Fruit Salad 70
    Stracciatella Valentine's Heart 72
Acknowledgements 74
About the Author 75

Introduction

As winter approaches, we haul out our heavy sweaters and the hats and gloves and scarves that will protect us from the wind, snow and ice that will soon arrive. Even if Earth is actually at its closest to the sun during December, don't let the sunny days fool you: Not only will you need warm clothing, you'll also need some serious comfort food to get you through the chilliest months. When I say "comfort" food, I'm talking about delicious and good-for-your-body-and-mind recipes that will make your cold days happier, healthier and warmer. For this book, I've come up with a selection of dazzling recipes that should fit the bill!

Many people frown as the warm days draw to an end, but personally, I kind of like this time of year. With winter come so many wonderful vegetables and culinary specialties. If you've read my first cookbook, *Chef Q in Paris: The Fall Collection*, you know that for me, it's all about seasonal products. Growing up, I spent a lot of time on my grandparents' farm in the French countryside and got used to cooking with what was available at the time, at my grandmother's side. Seasonal products have everything going for them—including flavor and price. And winter has just as much to offer as the warmer months. Nature might look as if it's asleep, but when it comes to producing ingredients for our recipes, it's not! We can still have fun in the kitchen and enjoy great dishes this time of year.

From soup to stew, chocolate and fruit desserts to warm drinks, you'll find some of my most preferred recipes in this cookbook so that we can all spend these months—that often seem so long—armed with the best weapon at our disposal: FOOD! I'm not joking. Having a well-balanced diet throughout the winter can truly help you stay healthy and fight common viruses, and the special bonus is all of this great food will lift your spirits too. Therefore, I've focused on specific ingredients that are central to feeling good when the temperatures drop, and that make this an enjoyable season for your taste buds and your well-being.

My winter shopping list? Fill your shopping basket with color! Multicolor ingredients are the secret behind harmonious menus this winter. The following list is non-exhaustive, but it will give you an idea of where to start:
- Escarole
- Radicchio
- Belgian endive
- Sweet potato
- Celeriac
- Cabbage
- Brussels sprouts
- Red onion
- Squash (all of them!)
- Citrus
- Apples
- Pears

And… chocolate! Certain foods can stimulate the happy-making parts of your brain, and chocolate is definitely one of them. As for drinks, tea and coffee are fine in moderation, and remember to get plenty of water too. When it's cold outside, we don't feel as thirsty as we do the rest of the year, so keep an eye on that H2O level, and drink a few glasses a day.

Oh, one quick thing before you follow me into the kitchen. You will notice, as in my previous cookbook, that all measurements for my recipes are in ounces and fluid ounces (as well as converted into European measurements). My American clients often say "Please, Didier, convert this recipe into cup measurements!" Until I tell them my measurements make the recipe fail-proof! If I have one piece of advice for you, even if you don't cook very often, it's to invest in a simple, small digital scale. It's more precise than a cup measurement, so you're pretty much guaranteed to get the recipe right. Say goodbye to the fear of packing flour when making a cake or using a cup that doesn't correspond to the standard. Numbers don't lie, so get that scale out of your cabinet, gather your ingredients, and start cooking!

And make sure to check out my Valentine's Day section because you know me, food is all about LOVE!

Cheers!
Didier

Soups

Odette's French Onion Soup

French onion soup is usually served as a starter, right? Not where I come from! You see, my family followed the myth behind this soup quite closely. Legend has it that French onion soup was invented by King Louis XV, in the wee hours. During a hunting trip in the countryside, the king spent the night at his hunting lodge—but he soon realized the cupboards were bare, except for a few onions, some butter and… champagne! He cooked the onions in butter, added the champagne (my guess is he saved some to drink, but historians have not confirmed my take on that), and combined the three ingredients to create the first ever French onion soup.

So, my ancestors must be related to King Louis XV. Because we always serve French onion soup in the middle of the night, after a copious meal for a special event: birthday, anniversary, wedding, baptism, or any big get-together. The older generation, most often the grandmothers, would go to the kitchen, peel onions and prepare a soup with the leftover champagne and white wine (if any, obviously!), a bit of broth or stock that was always on hand, and *voilà*! The guys would slice the bread and shred the cheese, then toast rustic croutons in the fireplace. And perhaps add a dash of cognac to their bowls (as if they hadn't had enough already).

I clearly remember hating this soup until I was a young adult; onion soup in the middle of the night is an acquired taste. There are as many onion soup recipes as French families, but here's mine (actually, my grandma's), and you don't have to wait until midnight to try it!

Getting Started

4 servings

15 minutes preparation time

45 minutes cooking time

Ingredients

4 medium-sized yellow onions
2 tablespoons butter
1½ quarts (1.5 liters) beef stock (or water)
8 slices French country bread
5 oz. (150 grams) shredded Swiss cheese (*comté, gruyère, emmenthal* for instance)
2 teaspoons cognac (or brandy)
¼ teaspoon pepper
Salt to taste

Preparation

1. Peel four onions and chop them into small bits.
2. Put onions in a large pan on medium heat, add butter.
3. Cook until onions are caramelized, turning a medium brown color, stirring every 2-3 minutes to ensure they are evenly cooked.
4. Add beef stock, pepper and a bit of salt.
5. Cook soup on medium heat and simmer for about 30 minutes.

6. Place slices of bread on a sheet of parchment paper on a baking sheet.
7. Spread cheese evenly on slices and put them in the oven, under the grill, to toast (5 to 10 minutes depending on your oven), until cheese is melted and starts bubbling.
8. Place two slices of bread in each soup dish and pour boiling soup on top.
9. Add ½ teaspoon of cognac per dish and serve immediately.

Cheers!

If you're fighting a hangover, I'd say a glass of water! If not, a dry white wine of your choice.

Didier's Tips

You can deglaze the brown onions with a half glass of dry white wine before adding your beef stock or water for a more acidic flavor.

Potato & Bacon Soup

What is winter without soup? In fact, what is winter without potatoes? So let's combine both with this recipe rich in texture, rich in taste—and rich in your wallet since it's so inexpensive to make. This quick soup will please you as much with its simplicity as with its flavor.

The story behind this recipe comes from my grandmother. She was the queen of recycling food, using all the leftovers in easy last-minute lunches or dinners. In her generation, when you lived on a farm, you knew how to cook anything and make it tasty. For this recipe, she would gather the extra cooked potatoes from a previous meal, cook them again in water and add… (I hope you're ready for this one) chicken feet. No reason to panic, she would clean them first!

In my recipe, you can replace the chicken stock with chicken feet, though you might want to tell your guests *after* they're done eating.

This soup is synonymous with comfort food for me. My grandmother would serve a traditional chicken soup or this potato and bacon soup with homemade croutons whenever anyone had a cold or was simply feeling under the weather. Followed by a bowl of French *faisselle* (cottage cheese) with honey on top. When you woke up the next morning, you would be good as new!

Getting Started

4 servings

10 minutes preparation time

30 minutes cooking time

Ingredients

3 Idaho potatoes (1.5 lbs. or 700 g)
6 bacon strips
1 small onion
8.5 fl. oz. (250 ml) chicken stock
8.5 fl. oz. (250 ml) water
Croutons
Extra virgin olive oil
Salt and pepper to taste

Preparation

1 Peel and chop potatoes. Then boil potatoes in unsalted water for 15 minutes. Strain and set aside.

2 Sauté bacon in a large saucepan on medium heat until crispy. Remove and set aside.

3 Chop the onion and add to the same pan (keeping the bacon fat). Cook until softened, about 5 minutes.

4 Add chicken stock and water.

5 Add strained boiled potatoes, salt and pepper to taste, and

cook on medium heat until tender (about 10 minutes).

6 Add sautéed bacon, roughly chopped with a knife.

7 Use a hand mixer to break up potato and bacon until you obtain your preferred consistency (more or fewer chunks).

8 Serve immediately with large croutons drizzled with extra virgin olive oil.

Cheers!

A white Minervois or a red Gamay.

Didier's Tips

Add a couple varieties of chopped fresh herbs: chives, chervil, tarragon… and a generous handful of shredded cheddar cheese. Plus, don't forget a tablespoon of *crème fraîche* (or sour cream)!

The Ultimate Chicken Soup

Simple and inexpensive, this recipe will warm your stomach and your mood. You'll even enjoy the leftovers. Unless you're like me and go back for seconds and thirds!

In the U.S., chicken soup is a real institution. It's even touted by some studies as a means to fight off the common cold. But above all else, this recipe is a steaming mix of flavors. Healthy and low in fat, a big bowl of chicken soup equals a balanced meal for those long winter evenings.

Just like any countryside recipe, "no waste" was the number one rule for this one. Even when our hens were too old to lay eggs and too chewy to be roasted, we found a way: Boil the bird with veggies—for hours. (Don't worry, for once I'll give you a shortcut; my recipe uses a boneless chicken breast.)

Is chicken soup American or French? Considering that in sixteenth century France, King Henri IV's favorite meal was *poule au pot*, I might presume France invented the soup. *Poule au pot* basically involved boiling a whole hen for hours with all sorts of vegetables. It was then served in a large bowl. The king loved the recipe so much that he decided to make it the national dish under his reign.

Others say the Americans invented the recipe when Campbell's brought chicken soup and noodles together in the '30s with its famous Chicken Noodle Soup. And yet another story says the ancient Greeks introduced the combination of chicken and broth since they believed chicken soup cured everything from bed-wetting to leprosy. Much like the eternal debate over which came first, the chicken or the egg, we can't really determine who invented chicken soup. But whether you credit the French, the Americans or the Greeks, the result is the same: a delicious timeless soup!

Getting Started

4 servings

10 minutes preparation time

30 minutes cooking time

Ingredients

1 lb. (450 g) boneless chicken breast
1 tablespoon coarse salt
1 medium-sized sweet onion
3 celery stalks
3 carrots
¼ lb. (110 g) pastina (or any type of little pasta)
8 cherry tomatoes, cut in 4
1 handful chopped Italian parsley
Pepper to taste

Preparation

1. Place whole chicken breast in a large casserole pan with about 2 quarts (2 liters) of cold water and coarse salt.
2. Bring to a boil on high heat and skim the top to remove foam.
3. When clear, cover and boil for 20 minutes on medium heat. Remove meat, set aside on a dish.
4. Finely chop onion, and chop celery and carrots into ¼-inch (0.5 cm) pieces. Add to stock, cover and cook for 5 minutes

on medium heat.

5 In the meantime, chop cooked chicken breast into ½-inch (1 cm) chunks.

6 Add pastina and pieces of chicken breast to stock, bring to a boil, cover and turn off heat.

7 Let rest for 5 minutes, add chopped tomatoes and parsley, and serve immediately.

Cheers!

A sémillon (white dry Bordeaux): light aromas of toasted almond, honey and green apple; round and medium-bodied.

Didier's Tips

Sprinkle a couple of tablespoons of grated parmesan cheese on top for an extra kick!

Cream of Parsnip

I'll give you a few hints: a creamy white color, a relative of the carrot as well as a sibling of parsley, a traditional veggie that is back in style… Have you guessed the star of this awesome winter soup? Your guests might not be so lucky playing my game! Since the scent of parsnip is almost impossible to identify and describe, rare are those who will guess what you're concocting.

From September to March, parsnips can be a staple in your kitchen. I prefer to wait for winter, though, since these tuberous roots require cold weather to convert their starches into sugar and develop their flavors. Conclusion: A quick frost bite and your parsnips will be even better!

Fiber, vitamins, minerals and antioxidants are great, but let's focus on the taste of this unique vegetable, the slightly sweet side of our parsnip. Before cane sugar and sugar beets made their way to Europe, parsnip was used as a natural sweetener. Close your eyes, taste a raw slice, and be ready for a subtle blend of anise and banana—an incomparable delicate flavor.

How to choose them? Preferably small to medium size (the large ones are sometimes fibrous), firm, and without "whiskers" or discoloration (brown spots), which will indicate they are rotten or heading that way. And if you're fortunate enough to buy parsnips with their leaves still attached to the root, do not throw those away! Add them to a salad, or chop them like parsley or cilantro and sprinkle on a baked potato with a large dollop of *crème fraîche*, a drizzle of extra virgin olive oil, and salt and pepper.

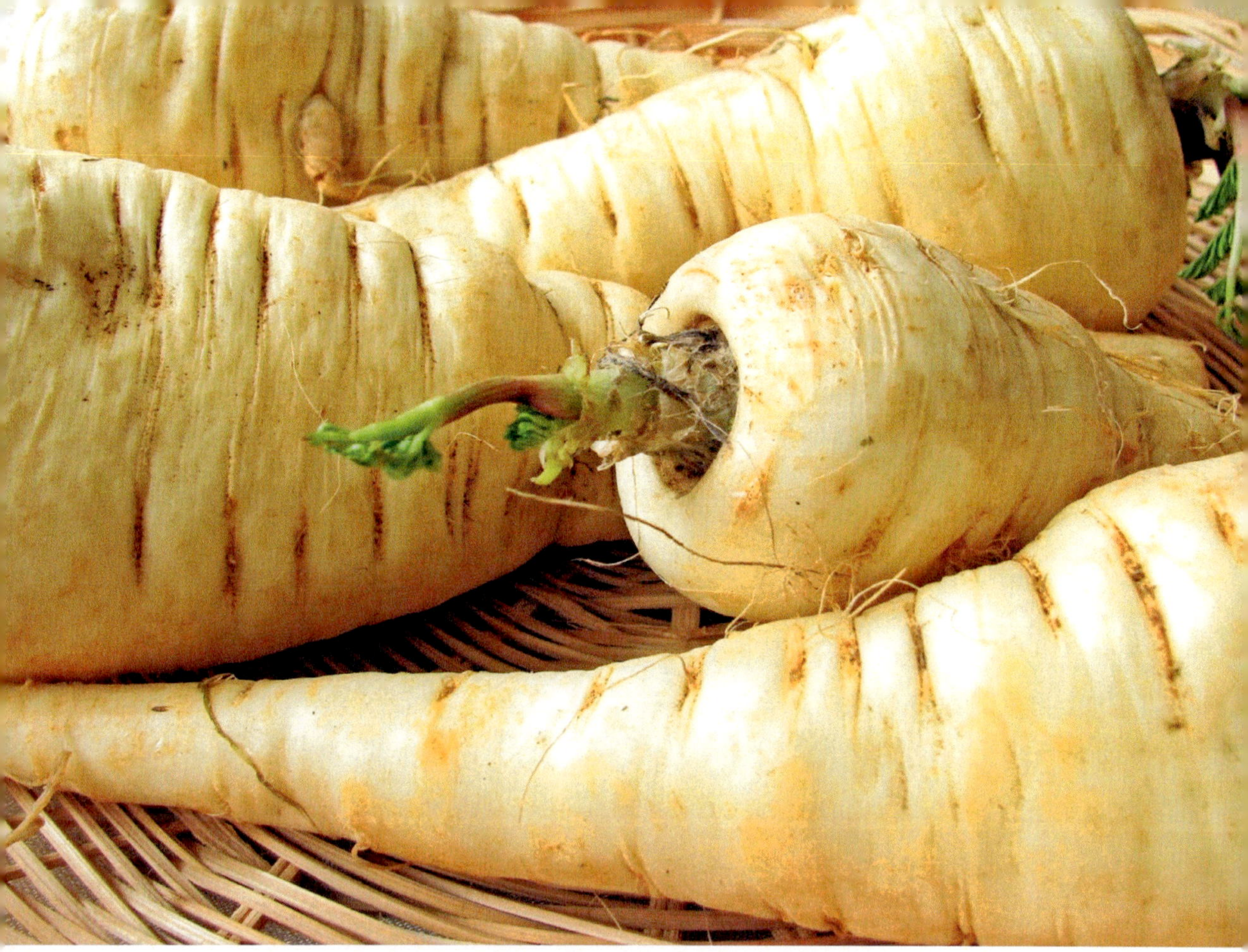

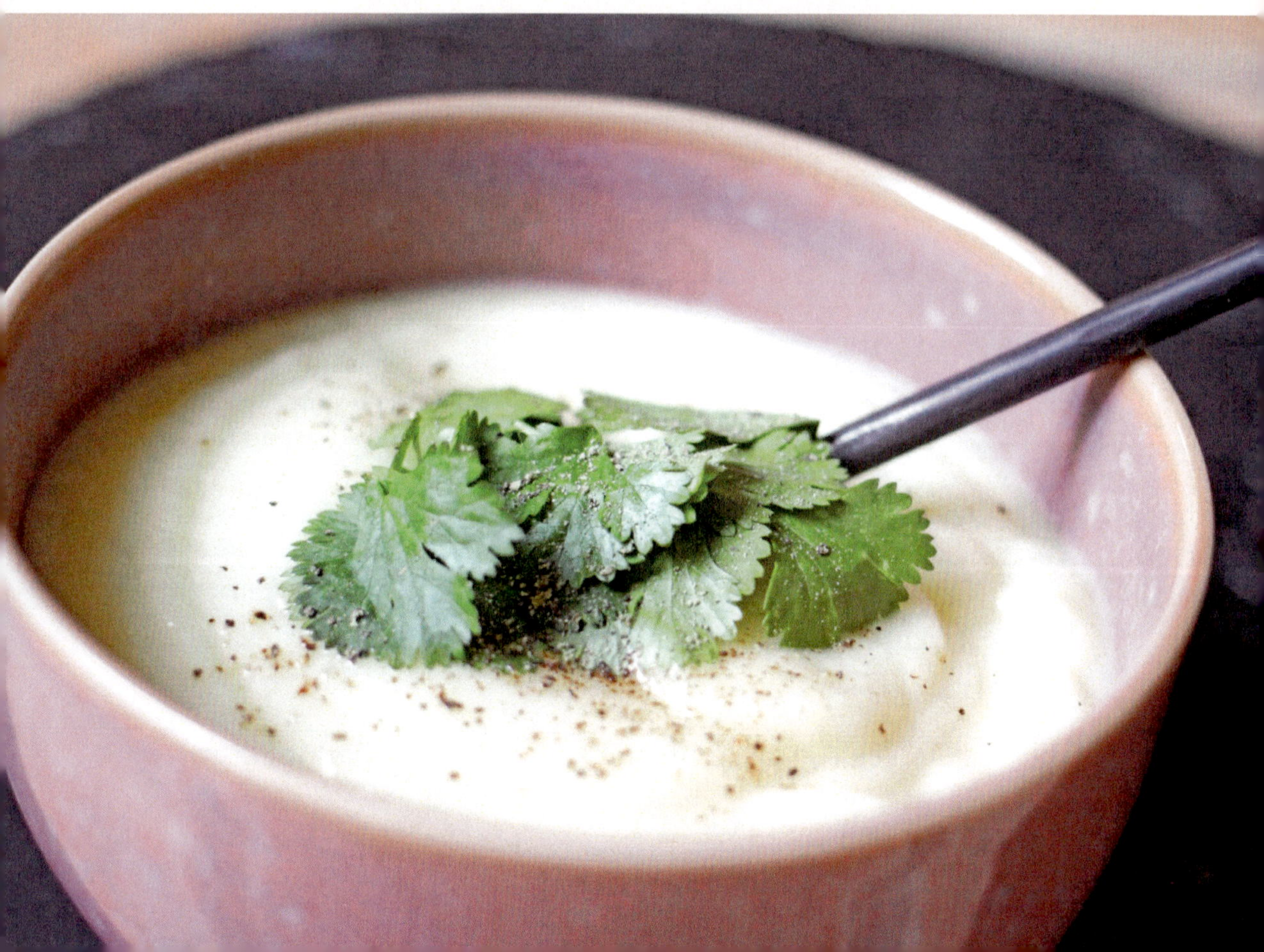

Getting Started

4 servings

10 minutes preparation time

20 minutes cooking time

Ingredients

3 medium-sized parsnips (2 lbs. or 900 g)
1 Idaho potato (½ lb. or 225 g)
½ tablespoon coarse salt
1 bunch fresh cilantro
4 tablespoons *crème fraîche* (if you can't find it, replace by heavy cream or sour cream)
Pepper to taste

Preparation

1. Cut ends of parsnips, then peel the parsnips as well as the potato and cut into cubes.
2. Place parsnip and potato cubes in a casserole pan and add water to the pan until the vegetables are just covered.
3. Add coarse salt and bring to a boil.
4. Cover and simmer for 20 minutes.
5. In the meantime, rinse cilantro, pat dry and remove leaves. Set leaves aside.
6. Mix vegetables (don't drain the water) with a handheld mixer and add *crème fraîche*. Stir.

7 Sprinkle with cilantro leaves and pepper.
8 Serve hot.

Cheers!

An aromatic and fruity Riesling from Alsace. The citrus and green apple aromas will delight you!

Didier's Tips

Chervil instead of cilantro, a dash of salted butter that slowly melts.

Main Courses

Turkey Breast with Normandy Cream Sauce

Let's take a quick trip to Normandy, where cream is *the* ingredient in every recipe (along with butter). *Escalopes de dinde à la Normande*, a classic in French cuisine, is a popular dish in all bistros, restaurants—and now in your home! In France, everyone knows this recipe. Still, sometimes it's best to go back to the basics.

When you're a French kid raised in the countryside and your grandparents have a farm, there are many dishes you will be served several times a month according to what's available during the season. I didn't mind for two reasons: I've always loved to eat, and when I like a recipe, I can eat it again and again. Even in the same week. This particular one used to be—and still is—in my top ten list.

What's not to like about it when you're a child? A tasty creamy sauce (for dunking big chunks of bread in), melted cheese and plenty of mashed potatoes! Now as an adult, I still close my eyes, forget about any diet, and splurge with pieces of baguette in the sauce every time. The only things I'm missing when I make this recipe today are the fresh cream my grandmother used to make from her cows' milk and the butter she would churn. Those provided the extra delicious notes to an always successful family-style meal.

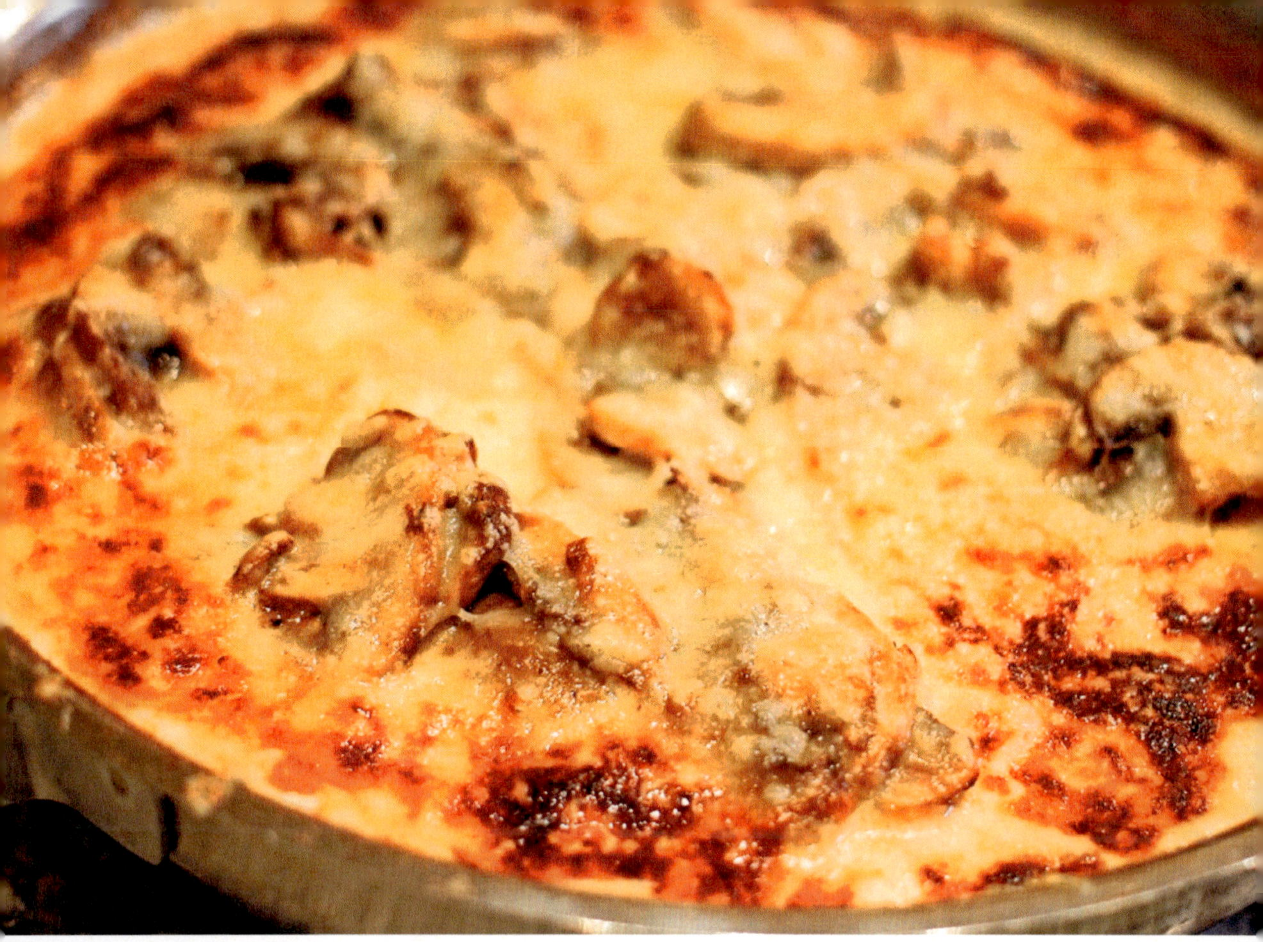
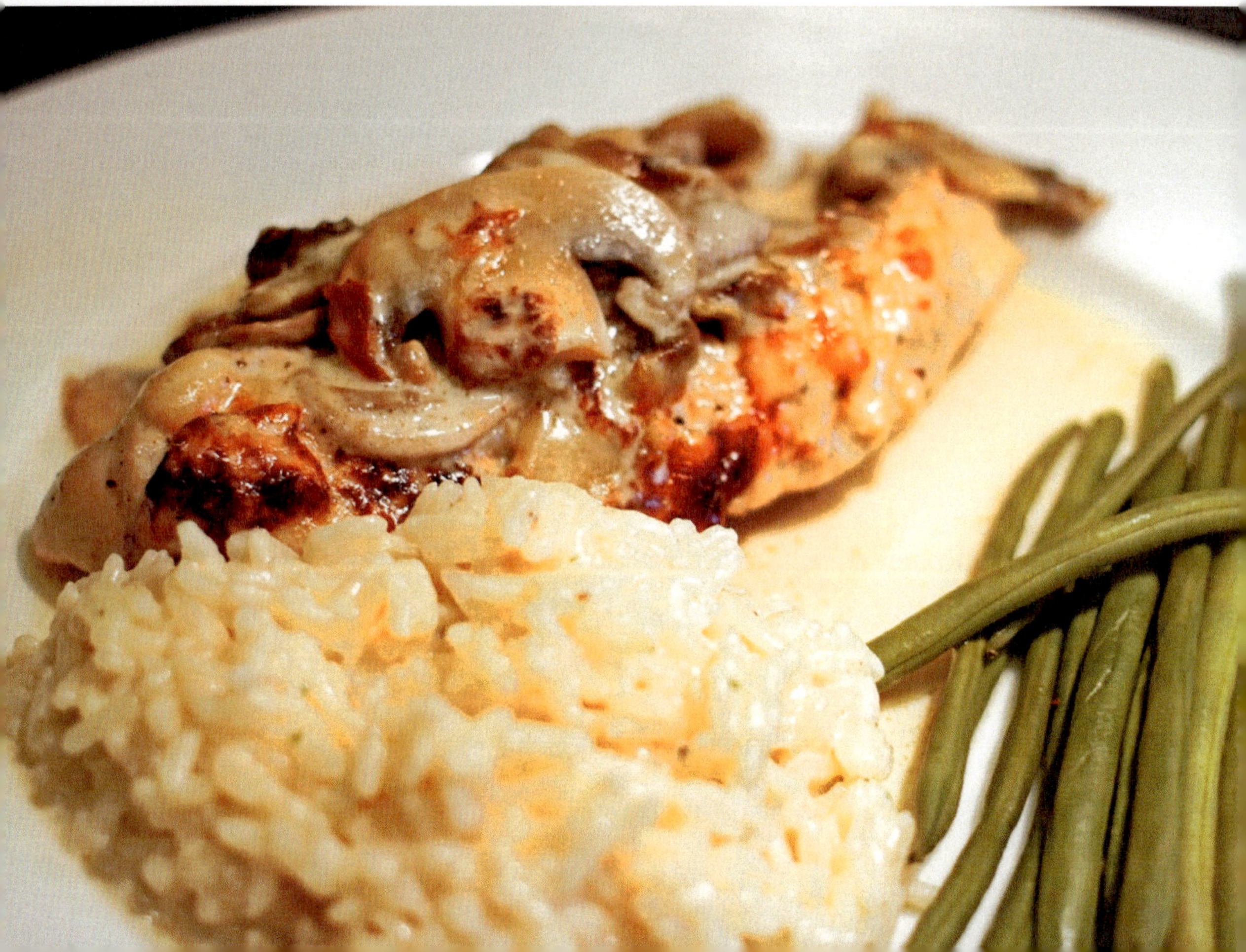

Getting Started

4 servings

10 minutes preparation time

30 minutes cooking time

Ingredients

4 thin turkey breast scaloppini, about 1 lb. (450 g)
1 tablespoon butter
½ lb. (250 g) fresh mushrooms
½ glass Marsala or port wine
12 oz. (340 g) *crème fraîche*
¼ teaspoon ground nutmeg
¼ lb. (125 g) shredded Swiss cheese (*comté, gruyère, emmenthal* for instance)
Salt and pepper to taste

Preparation

1. Preheat oven to 390 degrees (200 Celsius).
2. Cook turkey breast in a saucepan (the pan will go in the oven afterwards) on medium heat with butter.
3. Add salt and pepper and cook until slightly colored (about 5 minutes on each side). Set aside.
4. Slice mushrooms and add to saucepan on medium-high heat.
5. Add salt and pepper, stir and cook for about 10 minutes. Set mushrooms aside.

6. On medium heat, add Marsala or port wine, *crème fraîche*, nutmeg, salt and pepper.
7. Bring to a boil and let sauce thicken a bit (about 10 minutes).
8. Return turkey scaloppini to saucepan.
9. Top with mushrooms and cheese, and place in the oven for 10 minutes.
10. Serve immediately.

Cheers!

A hard cider from Normandy, a dry white wine (Sauvignon blanc) or a light red wine (Gamay).

Didier's Tips

Serve with rice, green beans, mashed potatoes… Your call!

Purée of Winter Veggies with a Twist

Squashes and celery root (the other name for celeriac) are everywhere this time of year, so it would be a shame to miss out! Rich in taste and texture, these veggies will power you right through the cold weather. They are filled with the nutrients essential to keep you healthy as the temperatures drop. These recipes can accompany your main courses or be served on their own.

My celeriac purée, simple and savory, will quickly become a regular at your table when you see how marvelously it teams up with any meat or fish.

And I've thrown in a second recipe, another classic with a little extra that will enhance everything: red kabocha squash purée with bacon. Red kabocha is flavorful like its green sibling, but sweeter. Its pale white stripes running from top to bottom make it easy to distinguish. Best of all? No need to peel it!

The touch of hazelnut oil and bacon in my recipes make the entire difference. Picky eaters, kids, and those who generally are not too keen on veggies will come back for more!

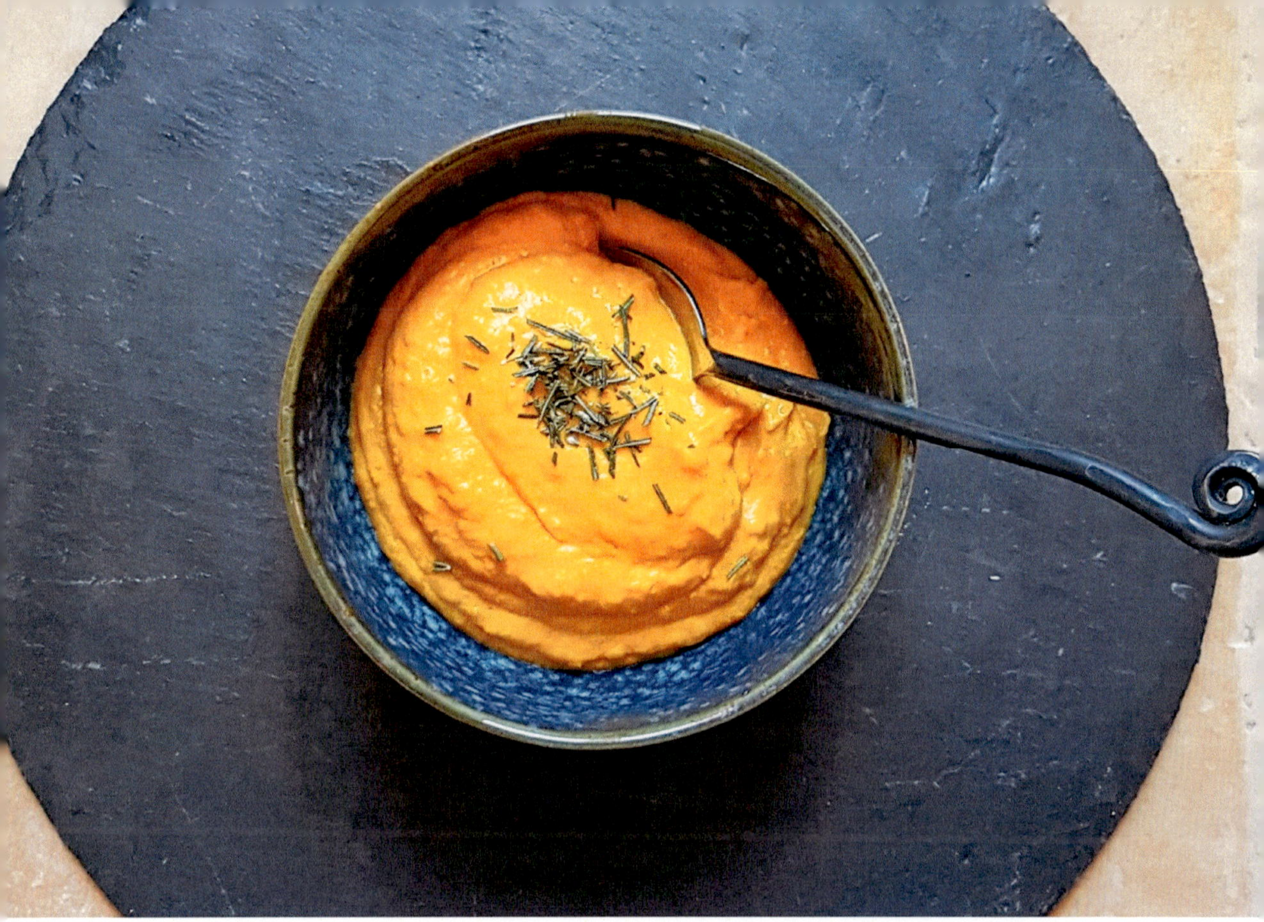

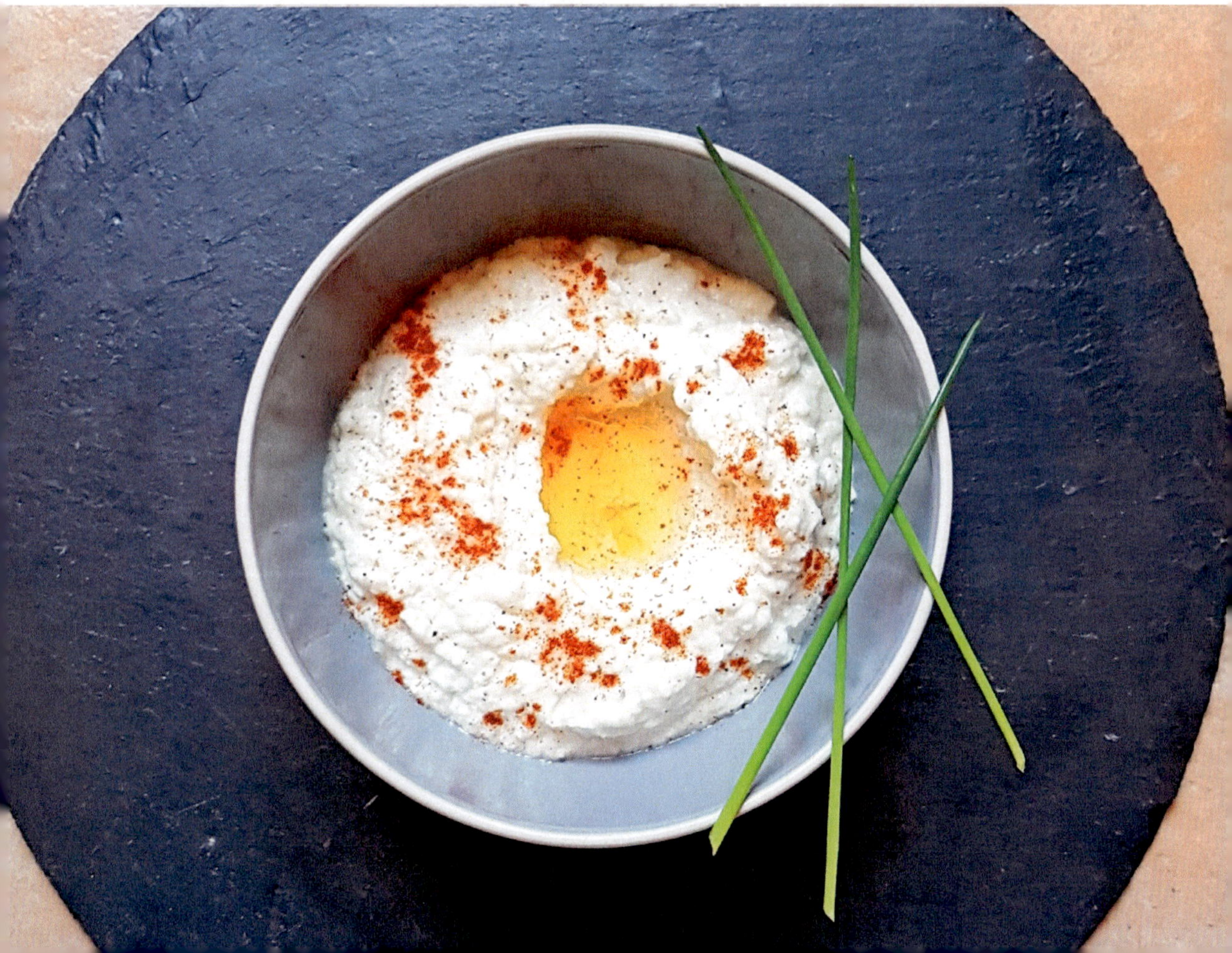

Celeriac Purée with Hazelnut Oil

Getting Started

6 servings

5 minutes preparation time

25 minutes cooking time

Ingredients

1 large celery root
1 quart milk (1 liter)
1 teaspoon coarse salt
3 tablespoons hazelnut oil
Salt, pepper and paprika to taste

Preparation

1. Peel celery root, wash, and cut in small chunks.
2. Place in a large saucepan and pour in milk.
3. Add coarse salt, cover and bring to a boil.
4. Reduce heat and simmer for 20 minutes. Celery is cooked when it's tender when inserting a knife.
5. Mix with a hand mixer, add two tablespoons hazelnut oil, and check seasoning.
6. Serve immediately with a drizzle of hazelnut oil on top, salt, pepper and a dash of paprika.

Cheers!

A nice Chardonnay from Burgundy: Chablis Grand Cru Grenouilles, for instance.

Didier's Tips

A pork roast will create the perfect combo! Check out the Roasted Ibérico Pork Loin recipe in my book *Chef Q in Paris: The Fall Collection*.

Red Kabocha Squash Purée with Bacon

Getting Started

6 servings

5 minutes preparation time

30 minutes cooking time

Ingredients

1 medium-sized red kabocha squash
2 small shallots
¼ lb. (about 125 g) bacon
2 tablespoons unsalted butter
1 teaspoon coarse salt
5 fl. oz. (150 ml) heavy cream
1 pinch chopped fresh rosemary
Salt and pepper to taste

Preparation

1. Wash the red kabocha squash thoroughly and cut in medium-size chunks, removing seeds. Peel shallots and cut in quarters. Mince bacon.

2. Place kabocha, bacon, shallots and butter in a large saucepan. Cook on medium heat for 5 minutes.
3. Cover with water, add coarse salt and bring to a boil.
4. Reduce heat and simmer for 20 to 25 minutes. Squash is cooked when it's tender when inserting a knife.
5. Drain with a strainer to eliminate all water.
6. Return to saucepan and mix well with a hand mixer.
7. Add heavy cream, stir and check seasoning.
8. Serve immediately with a sprinkle of chopped fresh rosemary.

Cheers!

A Burgundy Pinot Noir.

Didier's Tips

Great with a grilled duck breast or pan-seared turbot fillet.

Beer Lamb Stew

This is my go-to stew for long winter days, primarily because I love lamb. It's by far my favorite meat since it's so versatile. The second main ingredient is beer. I'm not a big beer fan when it comes to drinking, but for cooking, it's perfect. Whether you're preparing a batter, or baking bread, brownies or gingerbread, there's a beer for everything!

For this stew I chose two different beers: Orval and Carolus Ambrio. They work like a charm. The richness of the sauce, the slight bitterness of the beers that offers almost a caramelized note… Be creative by varying the alcohol, but keep in mind that dark or amber beers will give you the tastiest result.

A hearty and traditional Irish lamb stew is best when refrigerated overnight and reheated the next day, as all the flavors will blend and intensify. And the same goes for this recipe. That is, if you're patient—not an easy task when your whole kitchen smells so good!

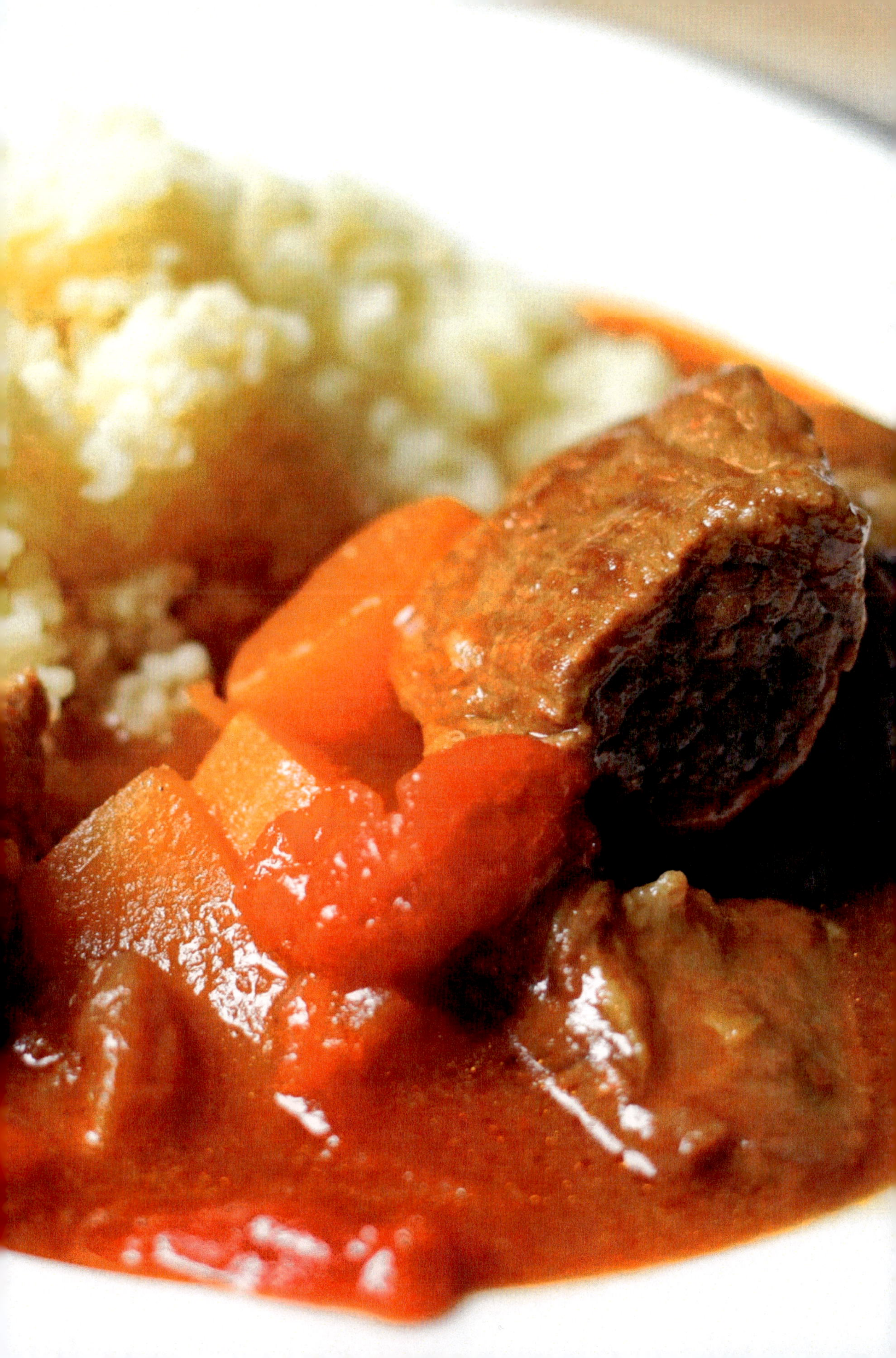

Getting Started

4 servings

15 minutes preparation time

90 minutes cooking time

Ingredients

2 lbs. (900 g) boneless lamb shoulder
3 teaspoons olive oil
1 shallot
2 garlic cloves
3 tablespoons flour
1 teaspoon Madras curry (powder)
1 quart (1 liter) dark or amber beer
1 can whole tomatoes (14 fl. oz. or 425 ml)
1 teaspoon tomato paste
1 medium-sized rutabaga, about ½ lb. (225 g)
4 carrots
1 handful raisins
½ lb. (about 250 g) semolina (couscous)
1 tablespoon unsalted butter
Salt and pepper to taste

Preparation

1. Cut meat into 12 pieces. In a large casserole pan, sauté meat over high heat with 2 tablespoons of olive oil until brown (about 10 minutes). Add a pinch of salt and pepper.
2. Mince the shallot, and peel the garlic and cut in half. Add to

the meat. Sprinkle with flour and cook for 5 minutes over medium heat.

3 Add curry powder. Gently pour in the beer. Stir with a wooden spoon and add can of tomatoes.

4 Add tomato paste and chunks of rutabaga, peeled and cut into quarters. Bring to a boil, cover and simmer over low heat for 1 hour.

5 Peel carrots and cut into ¼-inch slices (0.5 cm). Add to stew, along with raisins. Cook for 15 minutes, covered.

6 Place couscous in a bowl with a pinch of salt, a tablespoon of olive oil and butter. Bring water to a boil in sufficient quantity to cover the couscous. Pour boiling water over the couscous, stir with a fork and cover for 5 minutes.

7 Using a fork, stir couscous so that it does not stick. Serve a portion of couscous in a bowl with meat and vegetables. Drizzle generously with sauce and enjoy!

Cheers!

Beer, of course! Anything except white ale: Its flavors would be too light to compete with those in this recipe.

Didier's Tips

For a vegetarian version of this dish, replace meat with tofu (the cooking time will be 30 minutes).

Linguine with Butternut Squash

What's for dinner? Pasta. Again? Yes! I'm sure you've had this conversation in your house more than once. But I'm not talking about ordinary, boring pasta. This vegetarian recipe is simple, yet original and astonishing.

And you're going to love this: There are only four ingredients. Linguine, butternut squash, garlic and olive oil. It doesn't get much easier.

I discovered this family recipe on my first trip to the U.S., and it's still a favorite. What might seem like a strange combination at first will quickly become one of your preferred (and most popular with guests) vegetarian recipes. Try it, and you'll be hooked!

The story behind this combo is a traditional "don't offend your host and try to fit in" kind of deal. I was visiting my future mother-in-law for the first time, and I'd already struck out at breakfast. She'd asked if I wanted tea or coffee, so I replied politely (with the thickest French accent) that I'd take coffee. When she arrived at the table and started pouring, I said, "I'm sorry, I'll have coffee, not tea." The sweet woman looked at me as if I had two heads and replied, "Honey, this *is* coffee!" It was so weak I'd thought it was a pot of tea!

So at dinner that very same day, when she started spooning cooked squash on top of my linguine, I thought, "Don't say a word this time or you'll make a fool out of yourself again." When I saw everyone stirring the pasta and butternut together, I studiously did the same. And it was fantastic.

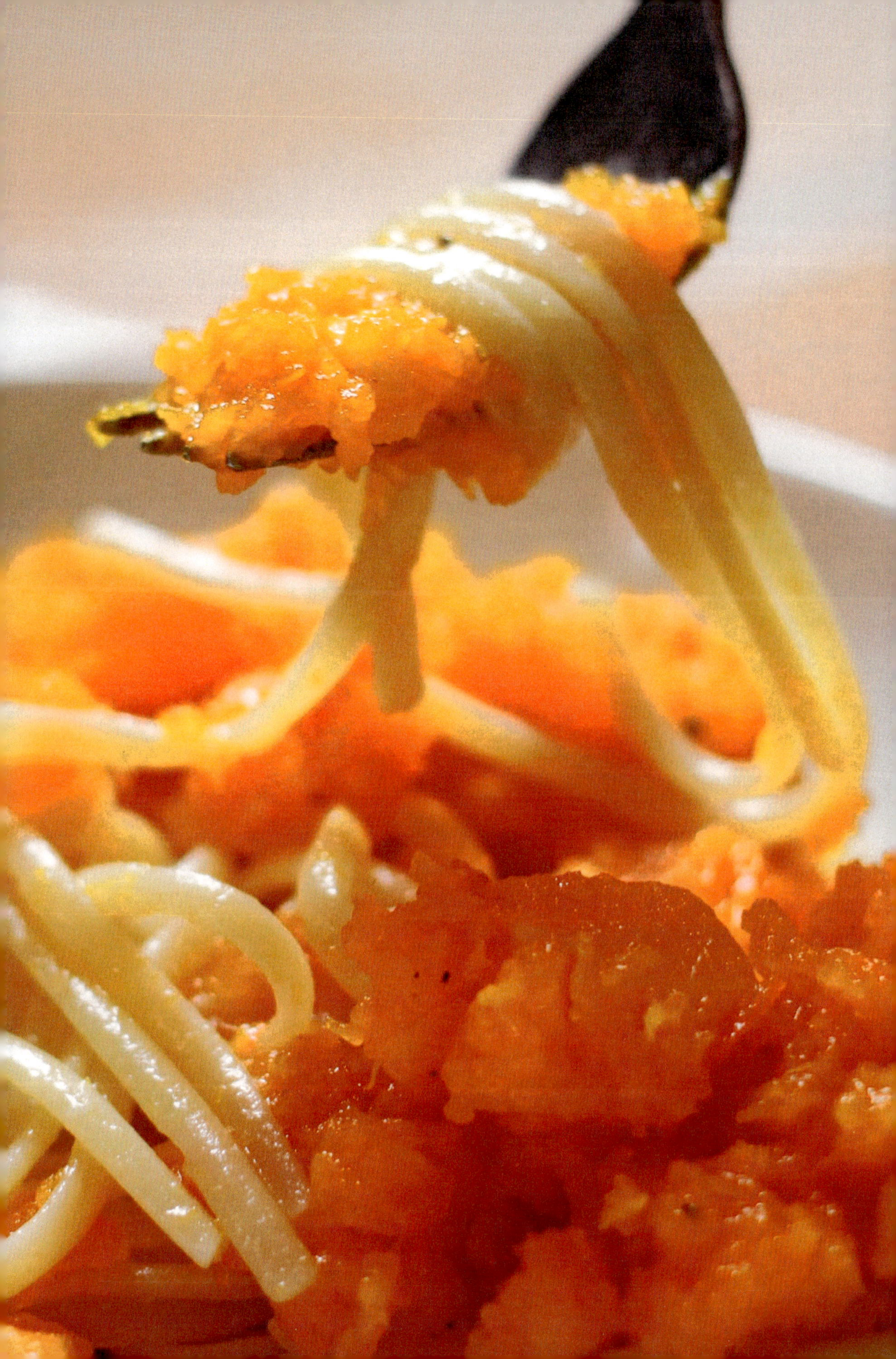

Getting Started

4 servings

5 minutes preparation time

20 minutes cooking time

Ingredients

1 medium-sized butternut squash, about 2 lbs. (900 g)
1 lb. (about 500 g) linguine
4 tablespoons olive oil
3 tablespoons coarse salt
2 garlic cloves
Salt and pepper to taste

Preparation

1 Peel butternut squash with a knife (be careful, the skin is hard!) and cut it lengthwise. Remove seeds with a spoon and discard. Cut squash into cubes, about 1 inch in size (2.5 cm).

2 Bring water for linguine to a boil.

3 Cook butternut squash in a skillet with 2 tablespoons olive oil over medium heat, adding a bit of salt, pepper and 2 tablespoons of water. Cover and cook for 15 to 20 minutes, tossing from time to time.

4 Add coarse salt to boiling water and cook linguine al dente.

5 Peel and chop garlic cloves. Add to butternut squash, cover and cook for another 5 minutes. The squash is cooked when

you can mash it with a fork.

6 Drain linguine and pour into a pasta bowl. Add 2 tablespoons olive oil to pasta and toss.

7 Serve pasta in dishes and add 3 to 4 generous tablespoons of cooked butternut squash on top.

8 Let your guests toss linguine and squash together as they enjoy their meal!

Cheers!

A dry white wine, a Cheverny for instance, or a white Beaujolais with white flower scents.

Didier's Tips

A handful of chopped Italian parsley on top of your butternut squash for a stronger flavor and burst of freshness!

Desserts & Drinks

Intense Chocolate Cake

A chocolate cake isn't all that original. There are thousands of recipes. But what if the top of your cake is crunchy and the center is moist? Still not convinced? Here's a little twist that makes all the difference: brown rice flour and corn starch. A surprising blend that will make your cake marvelously light. And without baking powder!

Let's pretend you're eating this dessert because it's good for you. Wouldn't that be nice? Well it's not too far from the truth. Brown rice flour is a nutritious alternative to regular flour (i.e., the one made from wheat) and is naturally gluten-free. It's high in protein, iron, fiber and vitamin B. It's also rich in manganese, which helps in the proper development of bones and cartilage. See? You're doing something good for your body by indulging yourself.

This recipe has a special place in my heart. A couple of years ago, when my daughter was old enough to give me a hand in the kitchen, this was the first cake we baked together. I'm sure she doesn't remember that day, but as both a chef and a dad, it was unforgettable. I'm pretty sure my kitchen counters remember it as well! I can't wait to teach her how to make soufflés and other fun recipes, but so far, with my daughter, it's all about chocolate. Sigh…

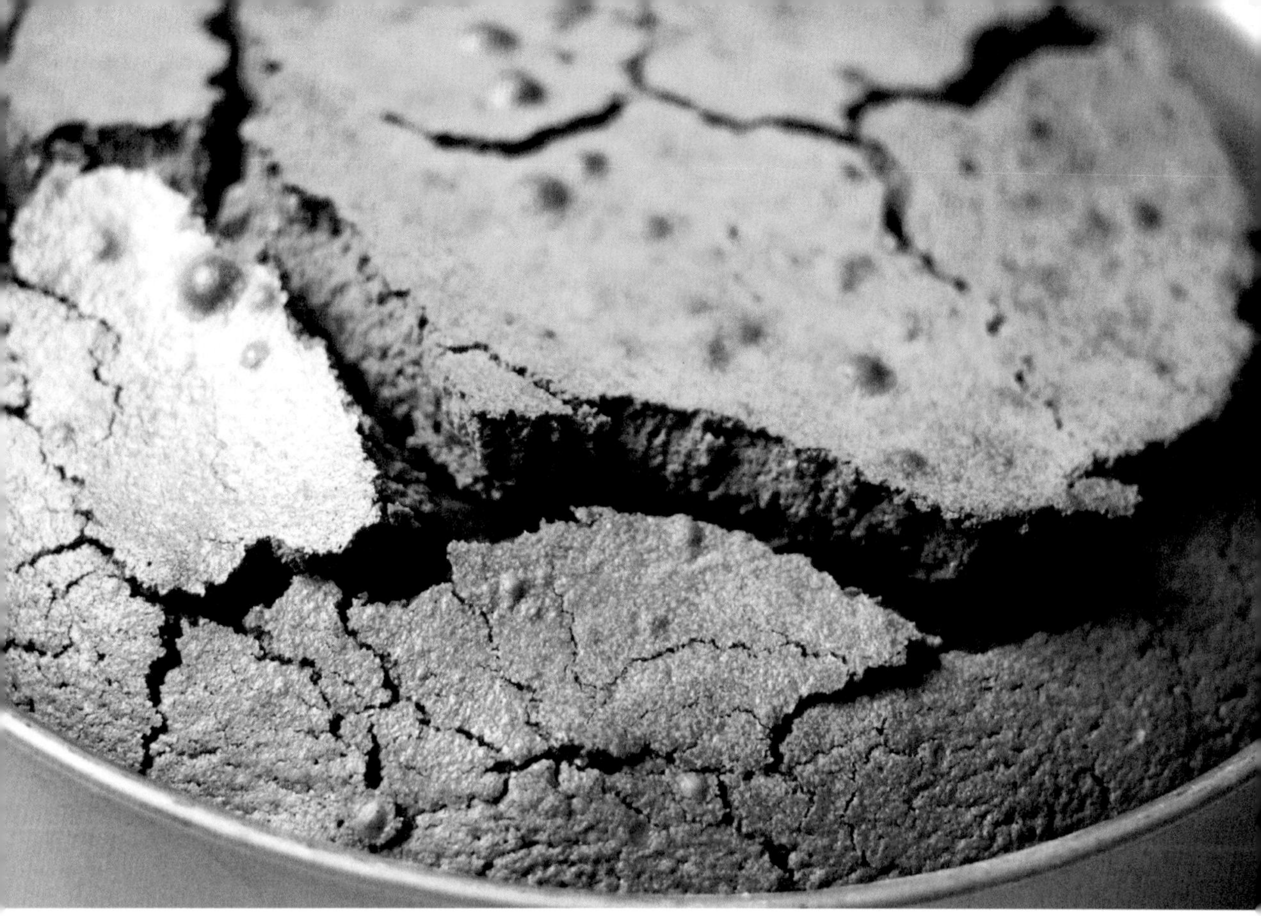

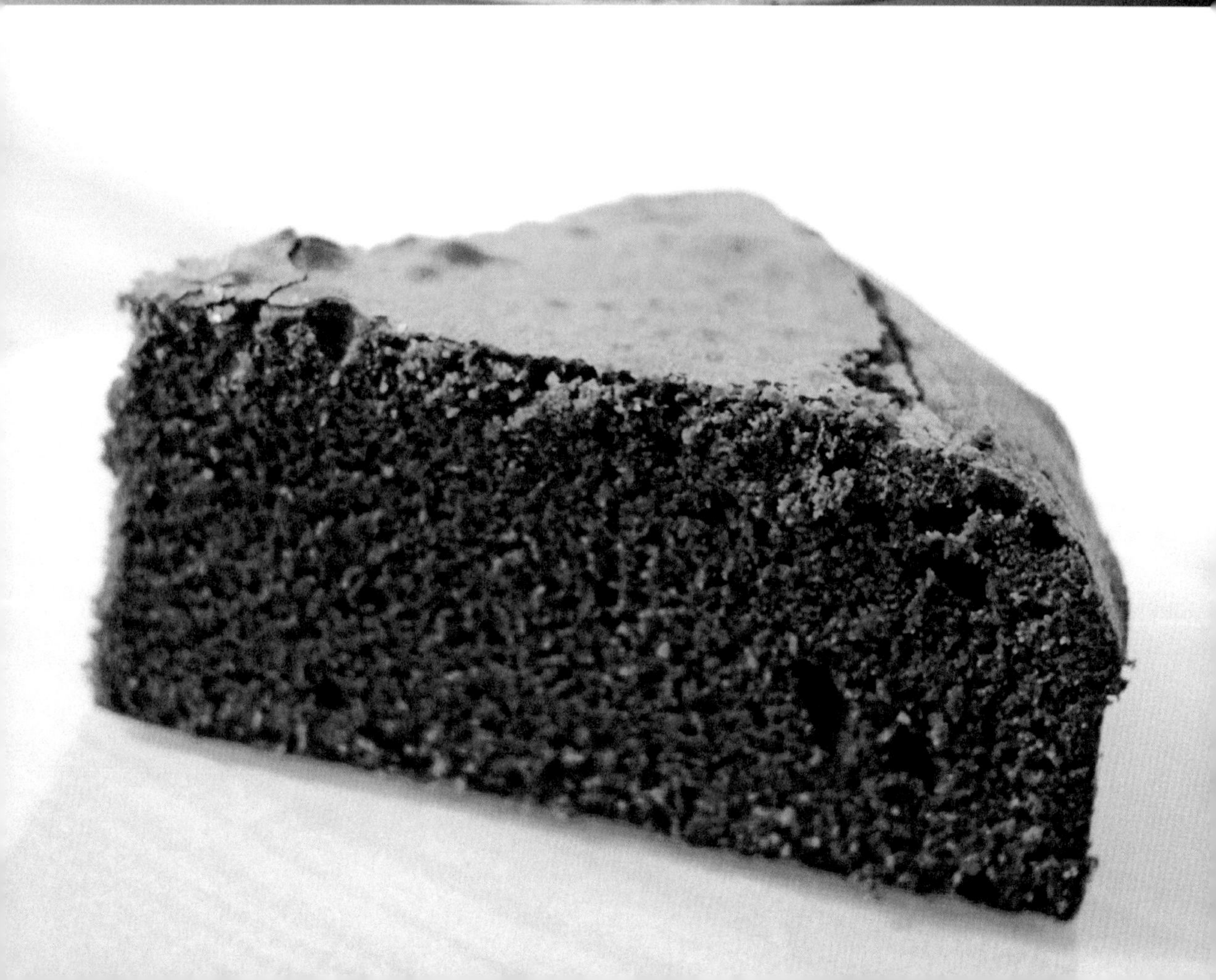

Getting Started

8 servings

10 minutes preparation time

40 minutes cooking time

Ingredients

9 oz. (250 g) unsalted butter
7 oz. (200 g) dark chocolate (minimum of 65% cocoa content)
7 oz. (200 g) milk chocolate
9 oz. (250 g) sugar
6 eggs
6 oz. (170 g) brown rice flour
2 oz. (60 g) corn starch
A dash of butter and flour for your cake pan

Preparation

1. Preheat oven to 350 degrees (175 Celsius).
2. On medium heat, in a saucepan, melt butter and both chocolates together. Stir well.
3. In a bowl, mix sugar and eggs and whisk for 3 to 4 minutes.
4. Add brown rice flour and corn starch. Mix well.
5. Pour in melted butter-chocolates and mix all ingredients thoroughly.
6. Grease and flour a 9-inch round cake pan and pour in batter.
7. Bake 40 to 45 minutes.

8 Remove cake from the oven, let set for 10 minutes, unmold and serve warm.

Cheers!

A good black coffee: a ristretto Grand Cru for instance.

Didier's Tips

A rich dark chocolate frosting on top or a scoop of vanilla ice cream to indulge even more!

Poached Pears in Red Wine and Spices

Poached fruit has always been a big deal in the French countryside where I grew up. When wintertime rolled around, my grandparents' farm was filled with all kinds of pears just waiting to be picked. Every year we would spend an excessive amount of time poaching them since they keep in the fridge for up to 10 days. It was also a good way for my grandmother, who ran a small daycare in her home, to get the little ones eating fruit. She would use only a few ingredients: water, sugar, vanilla bean and a splash of lemon juice. My recipe calls for wine, port wine and spices to poach your pears. A nice way to celebrate the holiday season!

For this recipe, I always choose the Comice variety. These pears are among the sweetest, and they also are juicy so they're technically not recommended for cooking. But for poaching, they are exactly what we need. They will stay moist, will release lots of flavors when poaching, and their creamy texture will enchant your palate! Comice pears come in various sizes, but they all have one thing in common. Their shape is unique, with a round body and a short perfectly-shaped neck. To determine when your pear is ripe, gently press into its neck. If it is slightly soft under the pressure of your fingertips, it's ready to eat.

Often referred to as the "Christmas Pear," the Comice is known officially as *Doyenné du Comice*. This French variety was born in the Loire region, mid-nineteenth century. Comice pears usually have green skin with a rosy blush. As they grow, the significant difference in daytime and nighttime temperatures gives this coloration to their skin.

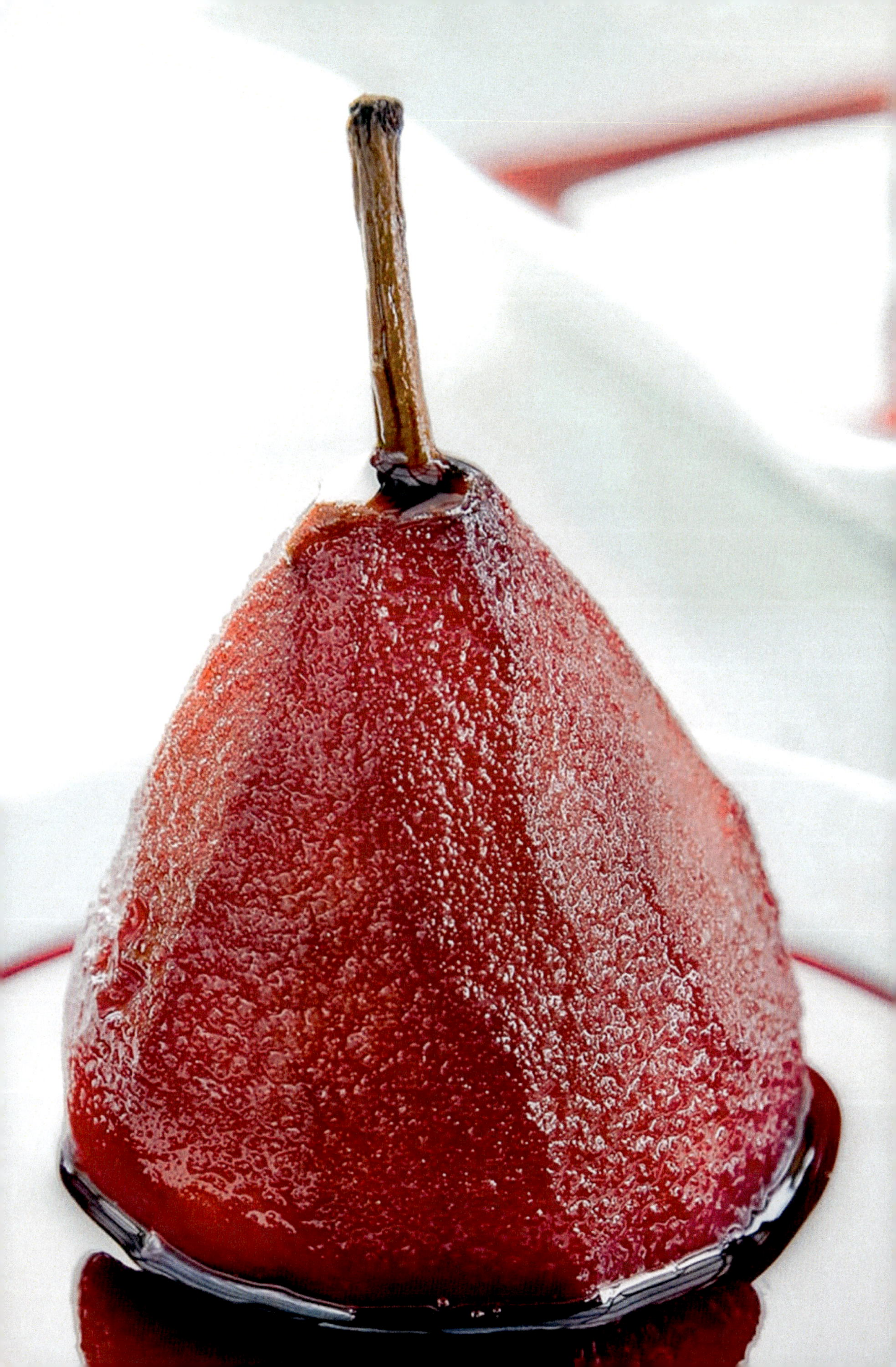

Getting Started

4 servings

10 minutes preparation time

30 minutes cooking time

12 hours refrigeration

Ingredients

4 Comice pears (choose them a bit firm and the same size if possible)
1 bottle of red wine (any red wine will do, so don't waste your best one!)
8.5 fl. oz. (250 ml) port wine
3.5 oz. (100 g) sugar
1 cinnamon stick (or 1 teaspoon ground cinnamon)
2 cloves
5 black peppercorns (optional, can be substituted with a few twists of your peppermill)
1 chunk of fresh ginger, thumb size
5 green cardamom seeds (or ½ teaspoon ground cardamom)
Fresh nutmeg (for the quantity, two swipes against your grater will do, or a very small pinch)
Zest of ½ lemon (organic)
Zest of ½ orange (organic)

Preparation

1 Peel pears.

2 In a large pan, bring wine and port wine to a boil over

medium heat.

3 Add sugar, cinnamon, cloves, peppercorns, ginger, cardamom, nutmeg and citrus zests.

4 Add peeled pears and poach in simmering heat for about 10 to 15 minutes, or until they are tender against the point of a knife all the way through the core.

5 Remove from heat and refrigerate for 12 hours.

6 Reheat on medium until the pears are warm, strain them, set aside in a dish and cover with foil.

7 Bring remaining juice in the pan to a boil and let reduce to obtain a syrupy consistency (about 5 to 10 minutes).

8 Serve pears in a dessert bowl and generously cover with syrup.

Cheers!

A Darjeeling green tea, smooth with a hint of sweetness.

Didier's Tips

Served with red meat, a turkey drumstick, seared foie gras or as dessert of course with vanilla ice cream or a few tablespoons of whipped cream.

Chocolate-Pralin Mini Bread Puddings

Pudding! A delightful little treat with a funny name. The word comes from the French *boudin*, and if you don't know what *boudin* means, consider yourself lucky. French *boudin noir* is blood sausage, but before you frown in disgust, let me reassure you. It's actually not that bad, with pork fat and onions to add some great flavor. Our *boudin* originally comes from the Latin *botellus*, meaning "small sausage," referring to encased meats used in Medieval European puddings—for dessert!

Now that I think about it, I'm not sure if all this talk about blood sausage is the best way to convince you to try these mini bread puddings. Here's an idea: Why don't you make this recipe and tell your guests the story behind puddings as you're serving them? Some might be reluctant to take a bite, and then you'll have more to yourself! Clever, isn't it?

Jokes aside, this chocolate-*pralin* bread pudding recipe is too good, too easy, and too hard to resist. Warm or cold with a little cinnamon whipped cream on top, and they are ready to go. They'll stay good in your fridge for up to 5 days, and you can quickly reheat them in the microwave before digging into the rich chocolate consistency.

Two important details regarding the ingredients:

First, I choose Valrhona chocolate (milk and dark). You must select a high quality chocolate for this recipe since it's the main ingredient.

Secondly, you'll need some *pralin*. You can find it in gourmet shops and sometimes in supermarkets. *Pralin* is a mix of crushed caramelized nuts (almonds and hazelnuts). You can also make this recipe without it.

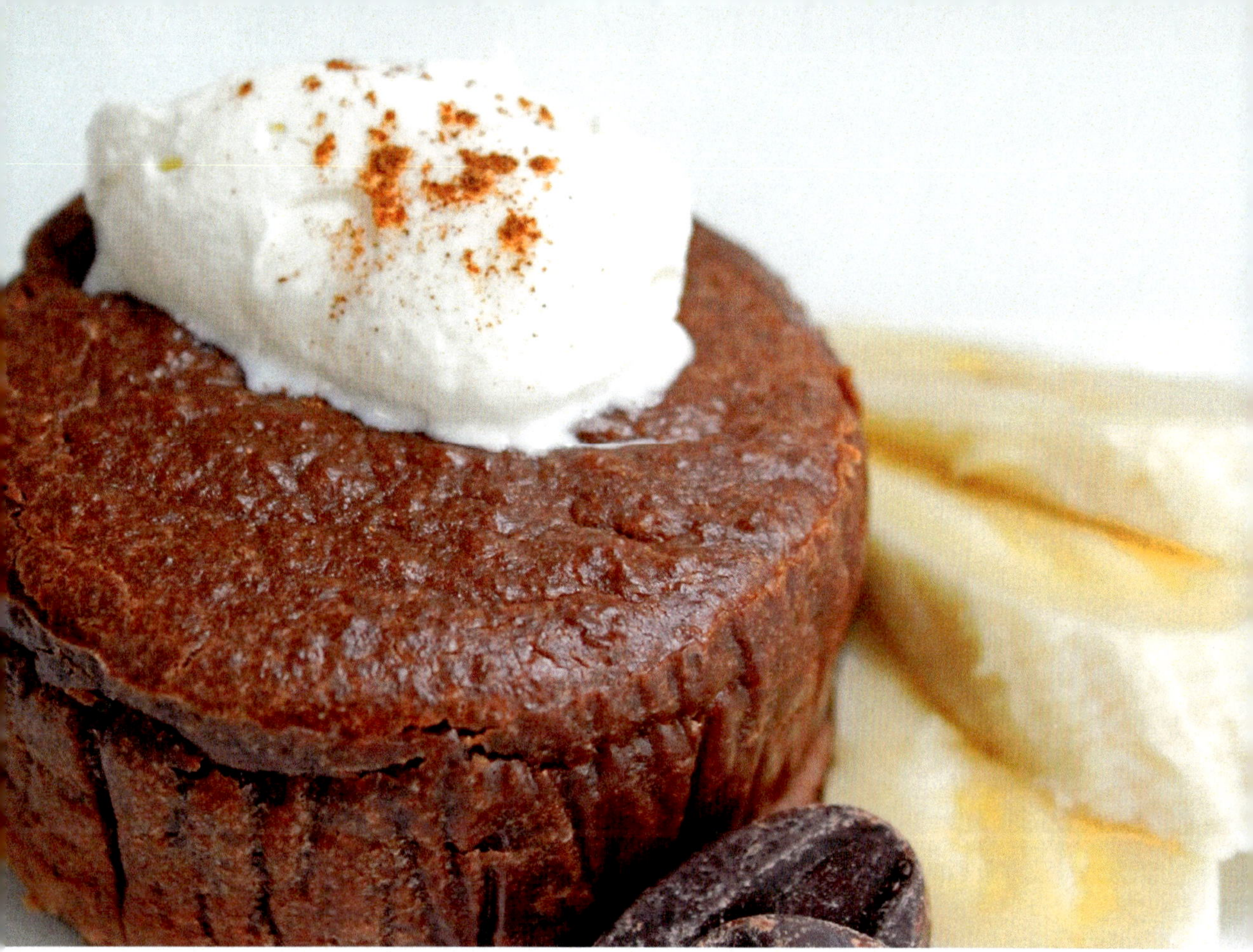

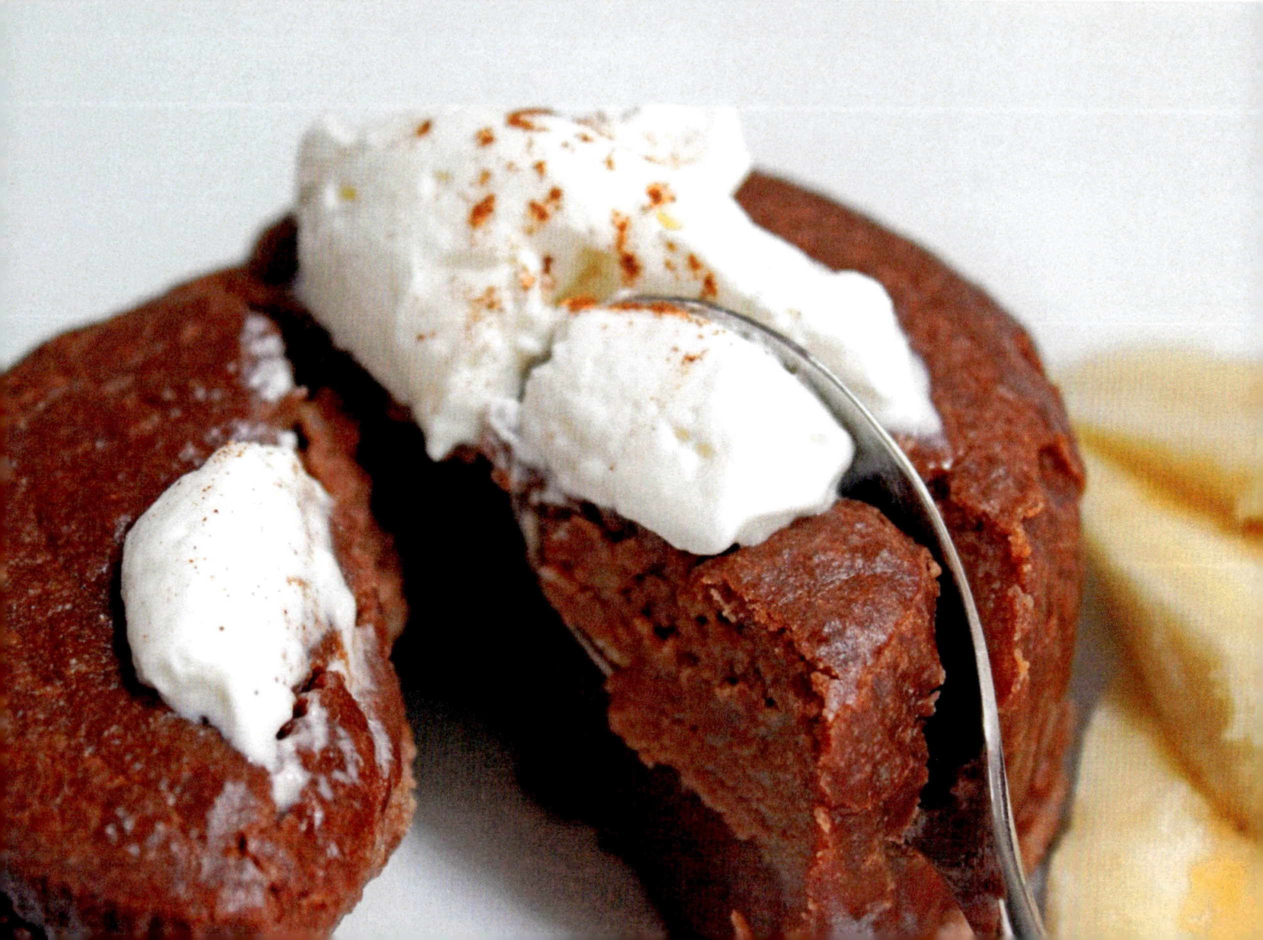

Getting Started

8 servings

20 minutes preparation time

30 minutes cooking time

Ingredients

1 quart (1 liter) whole milk
½ lb. (225 g) stale bread
2½ oz. (70 g) salted butter
4 oz. (120 g) sugar
3 eggs
1 oz. (30 g) unbleached flour
3 oz. (90 g) Valrhona Jivara 40% milk chocolate
3 oz. (90 g) Valrhona Guanaja 70% dark chocolate (70% cocoa content)
2 oz. (60 g) *pralin*
3½ fl. oz. (100 ml) heavy cream (very cold)
1 teaspoon powdered sugar
½ teaspoon cinnamon

Preparation

1 Preheat oven to 360 degrees (180 Celsius).
2 Bring milk to a boil, add stale bread and soften on low heat about ten minutes until milk is well absorbed and crust is soft. Add butter, let it melt and pour this mixture into a large bowl.
3 Add sugar, eggs and flour, and mix well using a handheld

4. Melt Valrhona chocolates (milk and dark) with *pralin* in a bain-marie (double-boiler). Add melted chocolates with *pralin* to the previous mixture. With a whisk (or using your handheld mixer), mix all ingredients thoroughly.
5. Pour into individual molds lined with baking paper (if you're not using silicone molds) and bake for 25 to 35 minutes, depending on the size of the molds. Test cooking time with a knife; the blade should come out with hardly any pieces sticking to it.
6. Serve warm or cold, with cinnamon whipped cream and a few banana slices. Refrigerate if not served immediately.
7. For the cinnamon whipped cream, whip heavy cream, adding powdered sugar and cinnamon.

Cheers!

A glass of Arcane Extraroma Grand Amber Rum from Mauritius. Smooth, with flavors of exotic fruit, chocolate, vanilla and dried fruit.

Didier's Tips

For a twist, add a small shot of dark rum to the mixture.

Chocolate Café Crème

Sometimes the best recipes are those created by accident. The perfect balance of acidity and sweetness from the coffee and chocolate in this recipe… well, let's just say I didn't exactly intend for that to happen!

You see, like a lot of people, I'm not much of a morning person. I need my daily dose of caffeine to clear away the early morning fogginess. Which means that on more than one occasion I've poured orange juice into my coffee (or vice versa).

On this particular morning, back in my teenage years, I'd prepared a delicious brunch for a friend. Everything was all set; it was just time to pour the drinks. I think you can see where this is going! One hot chocolate blended with one *café crème* later (and a little taste-testing to make it perfect) and *voilà*, this recipe was born.

It's like a liquid dessert—that you can enjoy any time of day!

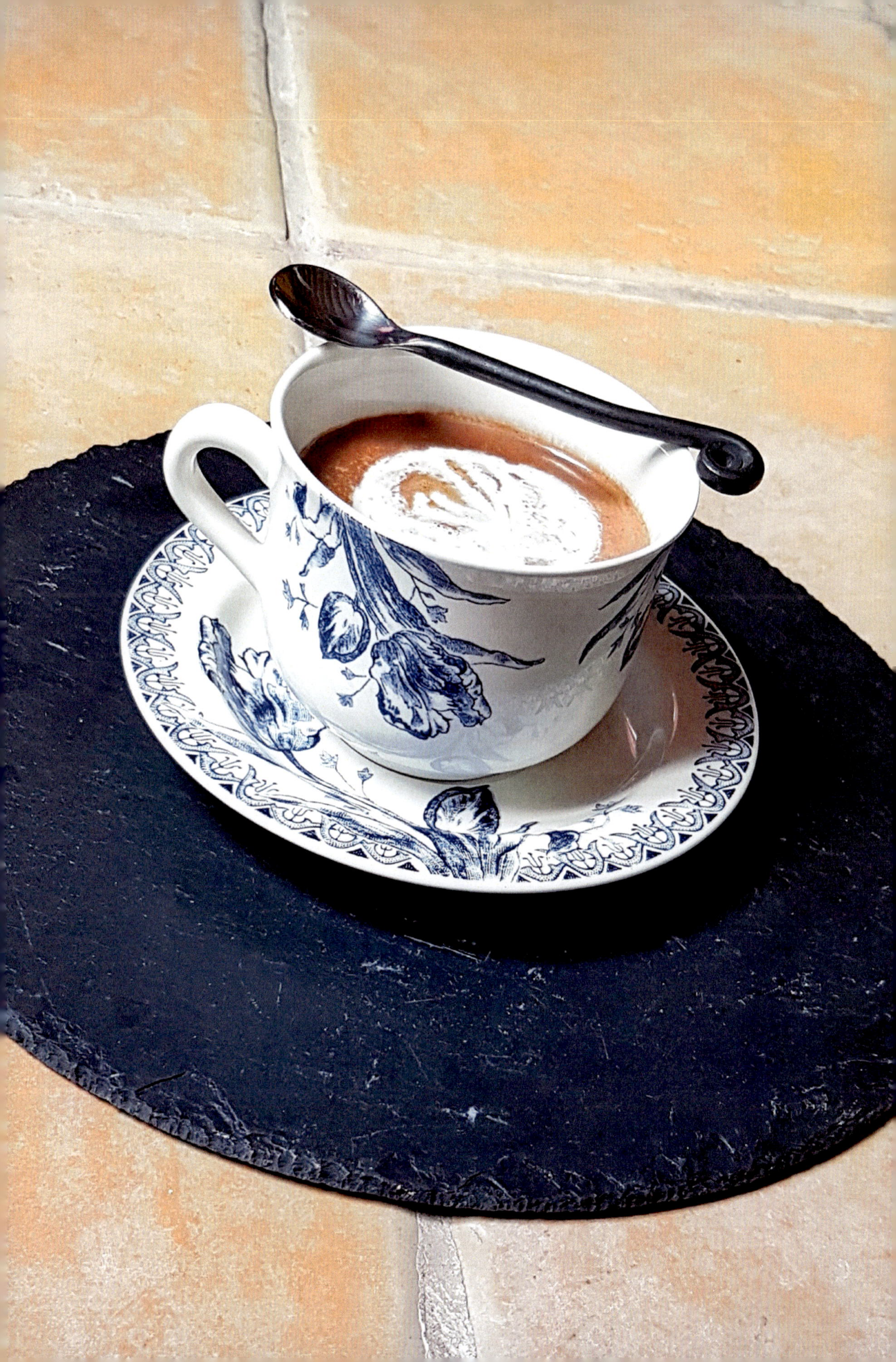

Getting Started

2 servings

10 minutes preparation time

10 minutes cooking time

Ingredients

2 fl. oz. (60 ml) freshly brewed strong coffee
17 fl. oz. (500 ml) 2% milk
3.5 oz. (100 g) dark chocolate (70% cocoa content)
1 vanilla bean, cut lengthwise
2 fl. oz. (60 ml) heavy cream, lukewarm
2 tablespoons brown sugar

Preparation

1. Brew coffee and set aside.
2. In a saucepan, melt dark chocolate in milk with vanilla bean on medium heat.
3. Mix with a wooden spoon. Bring to a simmer, reduce heat and cook 5 minutes while continuing to stir.
4. Pour hot coffee and hot chocolate into a teapot and let rest for 5 minutes.
5. Just before serving, add brown sugar and lukewarm heavy cream to teapot. Mix rapidly with a teaspoon and serve immediately. (Or chill and serve later for a cold drink).

Didier's Tips

For an extra burst of flavor, add a dollop of whipped cream on top, and sprinkle on a bit of unsweetened cocoa powder.

Traditional Hot Chocolate

Hot chocolate is a concentration of good stuff (it's high in magnesium and can help decrease stress and lower blood pressure) when it's consumed in moderation. Just a few sips will put you in a great mood.

However, its calorie and fat content are ridiculously high, at least if made with real milk or cream. So if you're going to indulge, make it worthwhile with my traditional hot chocolate recipe that only takes 10 minutes to prepare.

And if you really want to treat yourself, I say go all the way and add a dollop of whipped cream on top. Say *au revoir* to instant powdered drinks and *bonjour* to this decadent treat.

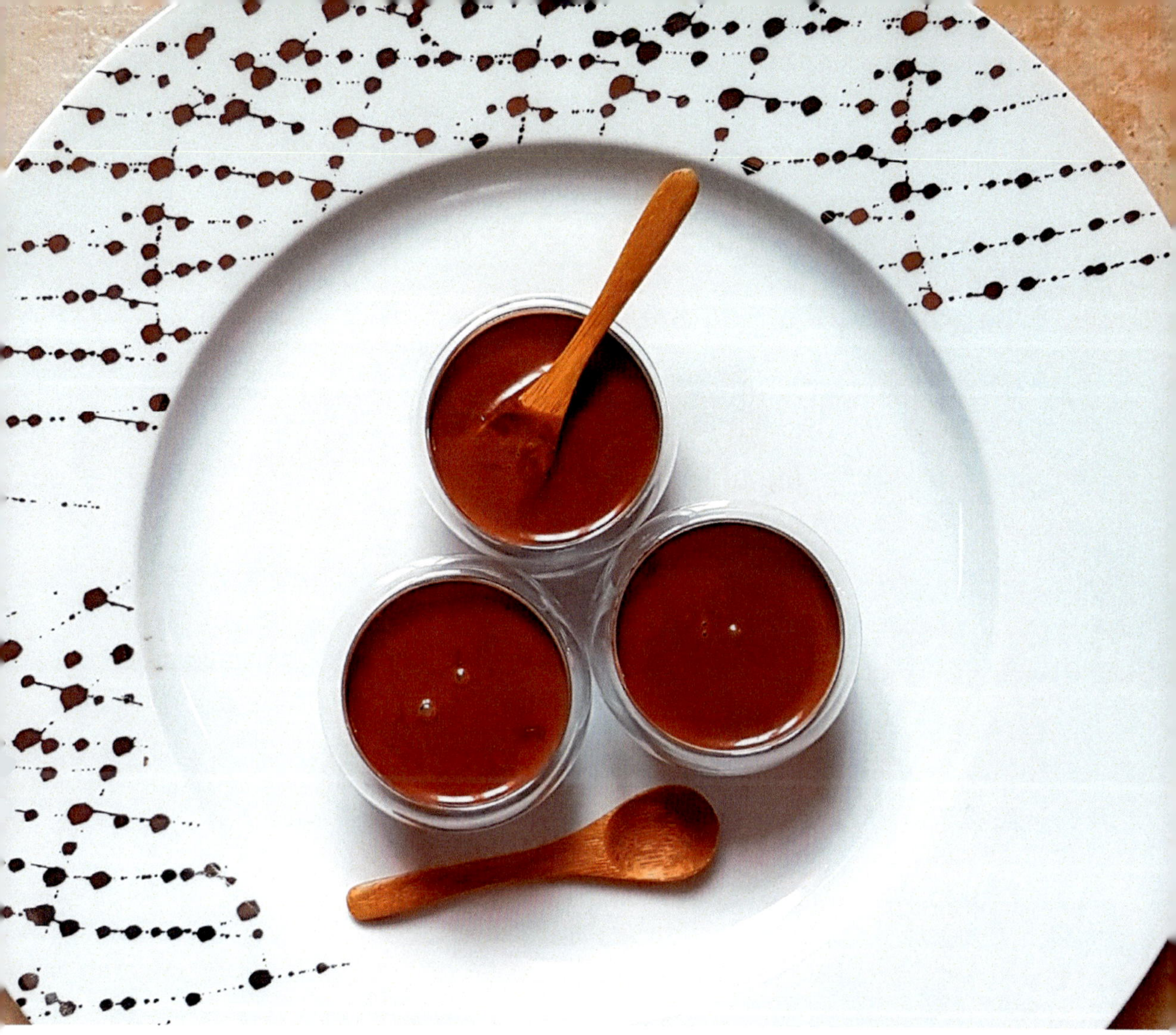

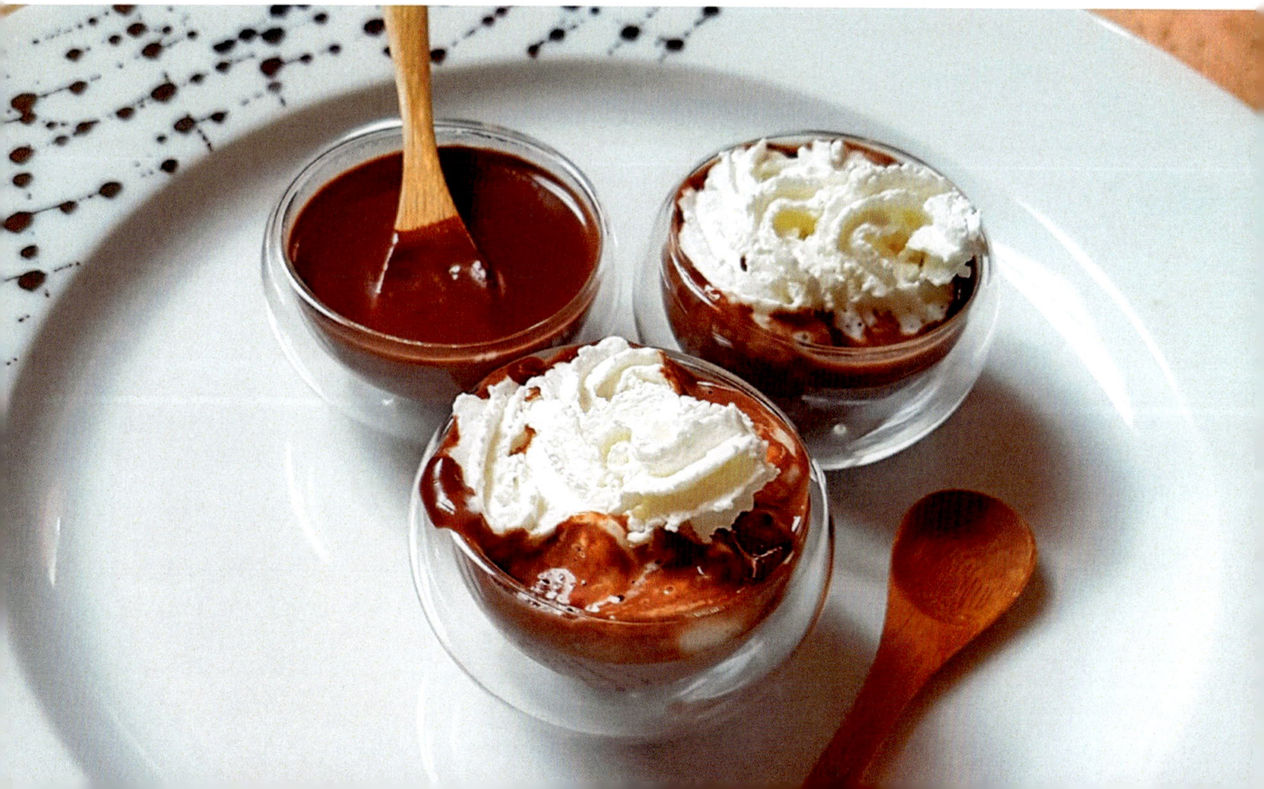

Getting Started

4 servings

5 minutes preparation time

5 minutes cooking time

Ingredients

17 fl. oz. (500 ml) whole milk
8.5 fl. oz. (250 ml) heavy cream
5 oz. (140 g) dark chocolate (70% cocoa content)
2 oz. (60 g) milk chocolate (30% to 40% cocoa content)
½ teaspoon unsweetened cocoa powder
1 pinch ground coffee

Preparation

1. In a saucepan, heat milk and cream on medium heat until boiling, then turn off heat.
2. Add chocolate pieces and mix with a whisk until melted.
3. Add cocoa powder and coffee.
4. Let rest five minutes and serve.

Didier's Tips

For those who like an even richer taste, I recommend placing all ingredients in a bowl and storing in the fridge for 12 hours. Then heat everything in a bain-marie (double-boiler) and whisk until completely melted. The slow infusion and the cold intensify the flavors. Remember: Never bring hot chocolate to a boil, and never reheat it directly on the burner or you will ruin the chocolate's delicate flavor.

And you can vary the types of chocolate for new flavors and sensations!

Which Tea for Your Macarons?

It's French, it's chic, and it's the perfect combo for a winter day. Tea and macarons love each other. For every flavor of macaron, there's a tea that's a perfect match. To aid your gustative experience, I've taste-tested numerous macarons and searched for the teas that most complement them. And let me say, there are worse ways to spend an afternoon!

Classic Macarons

Flavors: chocolate, coffee, vanilla, salted butter caramel, hazelnut, etc.

Possibilities: Darjeeling and Ceylon are the most well-known teas that would partner well with classic macarons. Or a Lapsang Souchong with smoky notes of European Spruce or Mediterranean Cypress for a striking contrast. Black teas are structured a bit like red wine, allowing an interesting transition between each bite of our sweet delicacies. Flavored teas also make a good match: spicy notes (cinnamon, cardamom, black pepper, cloves, ginger), floral notes (rose, jasmine) or those with essences like the bergamot in your classic Earl Grey, lemon or any other citrus.

My favorite: A black Irish tea with a slightly bittersweet aftertaste that marries well with all of your classic macarons.

Fruity Macarons

Flavors: lemon, grapefruit, pear, cherry, raspberry, mango, pistachio, etc.

Possibilities: Green teas take the top spot. They won't transform the taste of the fruit and will offer a touch of freshness to cut the sugary and sometimes pasty nature of fruity macarons. While Chinese green teas (leaves heated in basins) and Japanese green teas (steamed leaves) are vastly different, both varieties do the trick. Chinese Gunpowder (high in theine and rather astringent) and Japanese Sencha (strong in "green" notes) are great choices.

My favorites: Yu Zhu Chinese green tea, with notes of chestnut and pine, or Tamaryokucha Japanese green tea, which is both minty and buttery.

Flowery and Herbal Macarons

Flavors: rose, anise, orange flower, violet, poppy, mint, etc.

Possibilities: To avoid overpowering the subtle nature of these flavors, pair with white and yellow teas, semi-fermented teas (also known as blue teas) and post-fermented teas. These are exceptional, the *grands crus* in the world of tea! Oolong is a great choice.

My favorite: Without a doubt, a Pu-erh, a post-fermented variety that, like wine, grows better with time. Humid and earthy like autumn mushrooms and fallen leaves, one sip cleanses the palate and strikes a sharp contrast with the floral notes of your macarons.

The Perfect Valentine's Day Dinner

On February 14th, many of us would love a romantic, elegant dinner but without stressing out or spending too much time in the kitchen. My Valentine's day menu—a drink, an appetizer, a main course, a pre-dessert, and a dessert—makes that possible!

We'll start with a dazzling champagne cocktail to set the mood. Its notes alternate between slight bitterness, sweetness and acidity. The angostura (originally from Trinidad) reinforces the spicy, herbal and aromatic notes in this exotic beginning-of-meal drink. So without further ado, your menu for two:

Royal Passion

Ingredients

0.5 fl. oz. (15 ml) angostura
3 fl. oz. (90 ml) blackberry liqueur
1 fl. oz. (30 ml) passion fruit liqueur
8.5 fl. oz. (250 ml) champagne

Preparation

1. Pour all ingredients except champagne into a shaker with ice. Shake well.
2. Pour champagne into a flute. Add shaker's mixture of alcohols (hold back the ice) into the flute.

Apple Cheese Puff

10 minutes preparation time

20 minutes cooking time

Ingredients

2 oz. (60 g) camembert
1 apple
1 ready-to-bake puff pastry sheet
1 pinch cinnamon
1 oz. (30 g) melted salted butter
Salt and pepper to taste

Preparation

1. Preheat oven to 430 degrees (220 Celsius).
2. Cut camembert into 4 wedges. Peel, halve and core apple.
3. Roll out the puff pastry on parchment paper. Cut 4 circles: 2 of the same size and 2 others about 2 inches (5 cm) wider to cover the apple dome at the end of preparation. On the smaller circles, place a camembert wedge, sprinkle with salt and pepper, then top with an apple half to create a dome.
4. Top (each) with (the) last camembert wedge and a pinch of cinnamon, then cover with the wider circles of puff pastry.
5. Seal edges by pressing dough with your fingertips or a fork.
6. Melt butter, then brush on sealed pastries.
7. Bake 15-20 minutes. Wait 5 minutes before serving.

Roasted Hake with Potatoes & Sautéed Cherry Tomatoes

10 minutes preparation time

30 minutes cooking time

Ingredients

4 small Yukon gold potatoes
14 oz. (400 g) fresh hake (can substitute with halibut)
6 tablespoons olive oil
1 pinch smoked paprika
8 cherry tomatoes
1 handful chervil, chopped
Salt and pepper to taste

Preparation

1. Preheat oven to 465 degrees (240 Celsius).
2. Peel potatoes and steam for 20-30 minutes depending on size. If you don't have a steamer, boil for 20 minutes.
3. Place hake on a non-stick baking dish with 2 tablespoons of olive oil. Add salt, pepper and paprika. Bake for 20 minutes.
4. Sauté tomatoes in frying pan with 2 tablespoons of olive oil on high heat for 7-8 minutes, stirring occasionally. Add a bit of salt and pepper.
5. Arrange everything on a plate to share, drizzle potatoes with 2 tablespoons of olive oil, and top with chervil, salt and pepper.

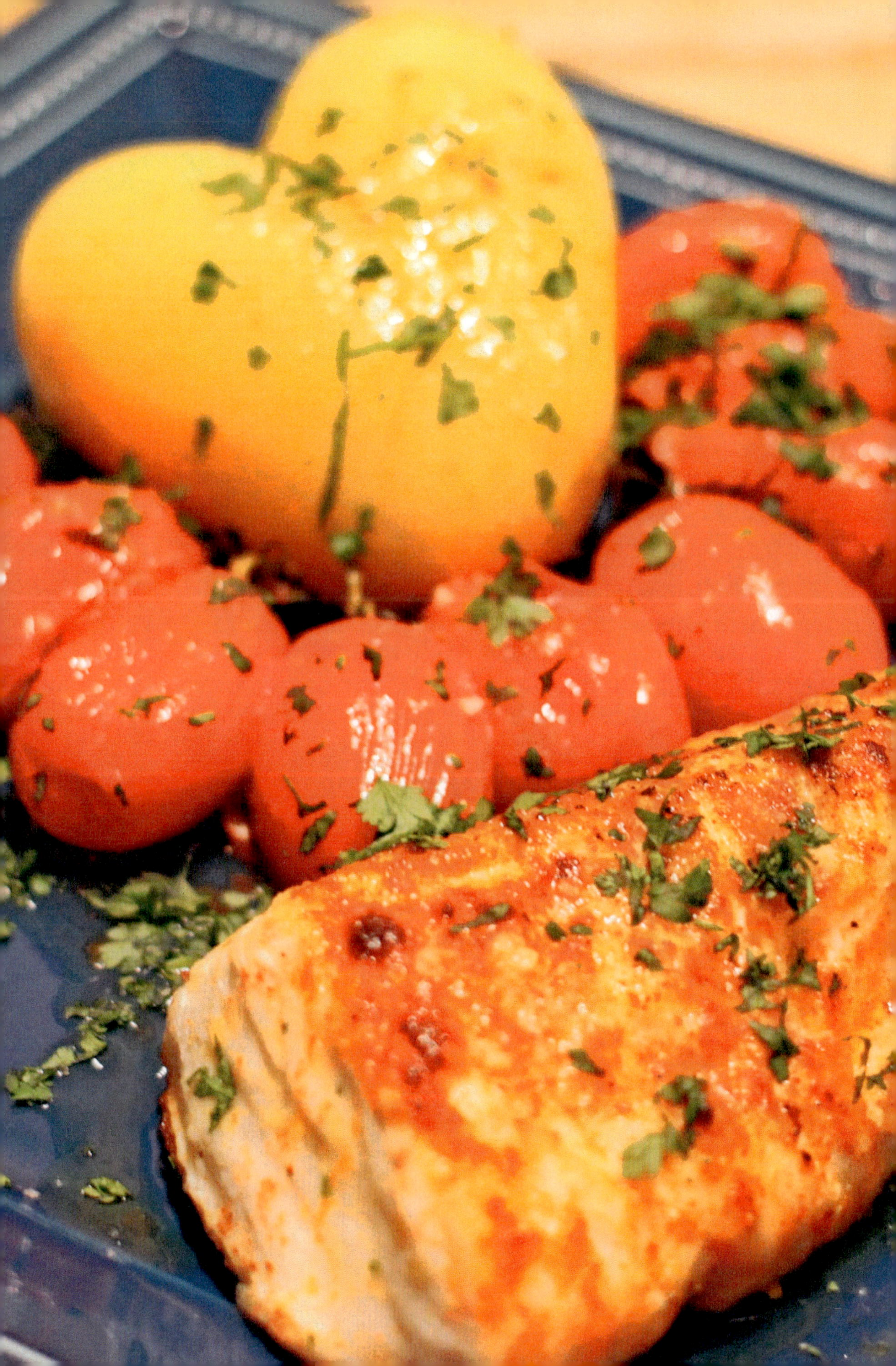

Champagne Fruit Salad

10 minutes preparation time

Ingredients

1 mango
1 kiwi
2 slices pineapple
2 oz. (60 g) blueberries
2 oz. (60 g) raspberries
12 red grapes
Juice of 1 orange (preferably blood orange)
7 fl. oz. (200 ml) champagne

Preparation

1. Peel mango and kiwi. Cut mango, kiwi and pineapple into cubes.
2. Gently mix in a deep dish. Add blueberries, raspberries, grapes and orange juice.
3. Pour chilled champagne over the fruit and enjoy!

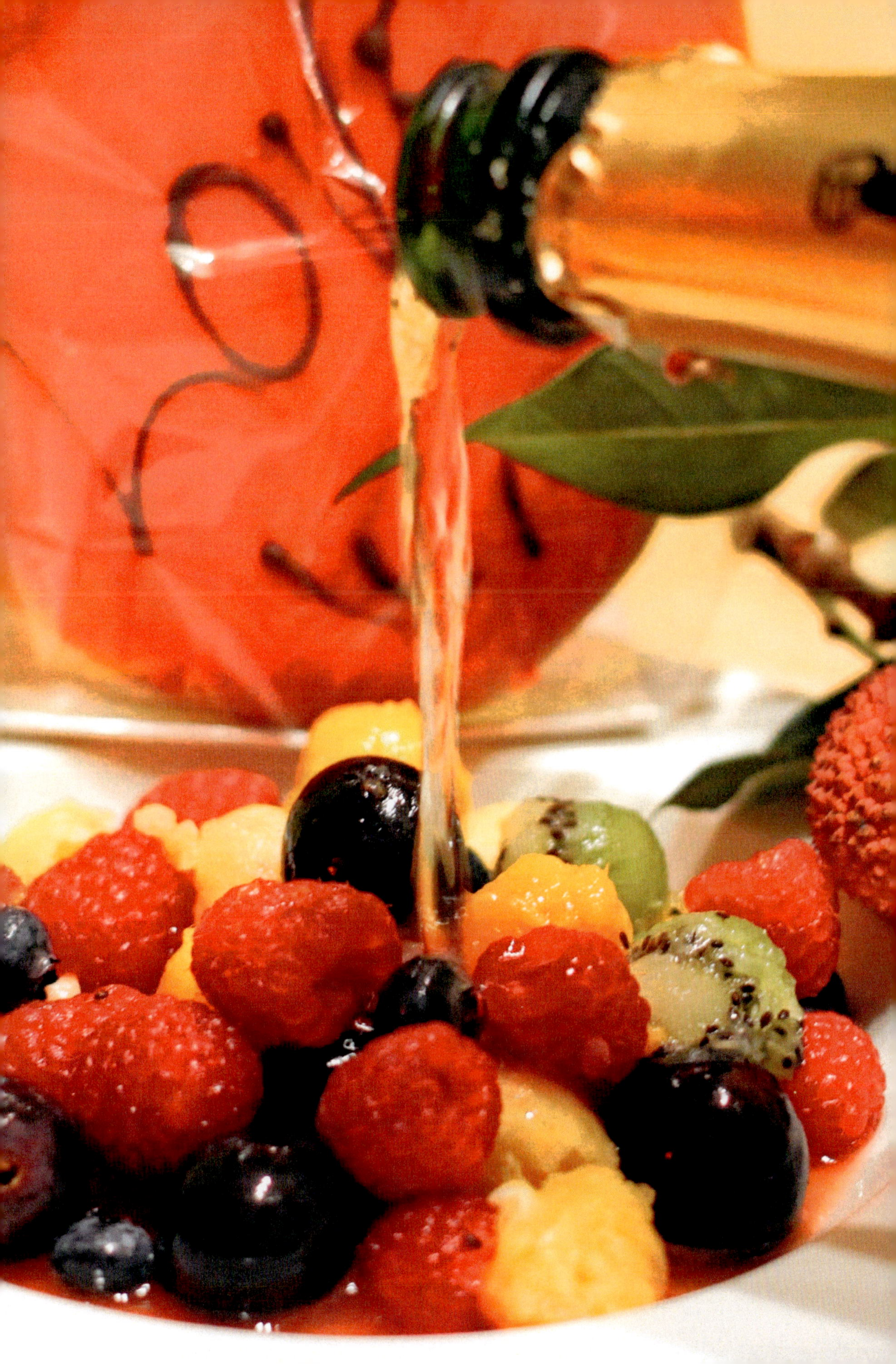

Stracciatella Valentine's Heart

10 minutes preparation time
20 minutes freezing time

Ingredients

1 large tablespoon mascarpone cheese
1 large tablespoon sour cream
1 large tablespoon *crème fraîche* (or cream cheese)
1 large tablespoon powdered sugar
½ teaspoon vanilla beans
2 tablespoons shredded dark chocolate
2 tablespoons roasted shredded hazelnuts
2 tablespoons red fruit coulis (or any red fruit jam)
2 tablespoons salted butter caramel sauce

Preparation

1. Combine mascarpone, sour cream, *crème fraîche*, powdered sugar and vanilla beans in small bowl. Whisk well. Add chocolate and whisk again.
2. Set a cookie cutter (heart-shaped is best!) on a dish, spread a bit of hazelnuts on the bottom, top with stracciatella mix, add a tablespoon of coulis, then add another layer of stracciatella.
3. Freeze for 20 minutes. Unmold gently and drizzle salted butter caramel sauce on top.

Didier's Tips

Replace hazelnuts with milk chocolate or white chocolate.

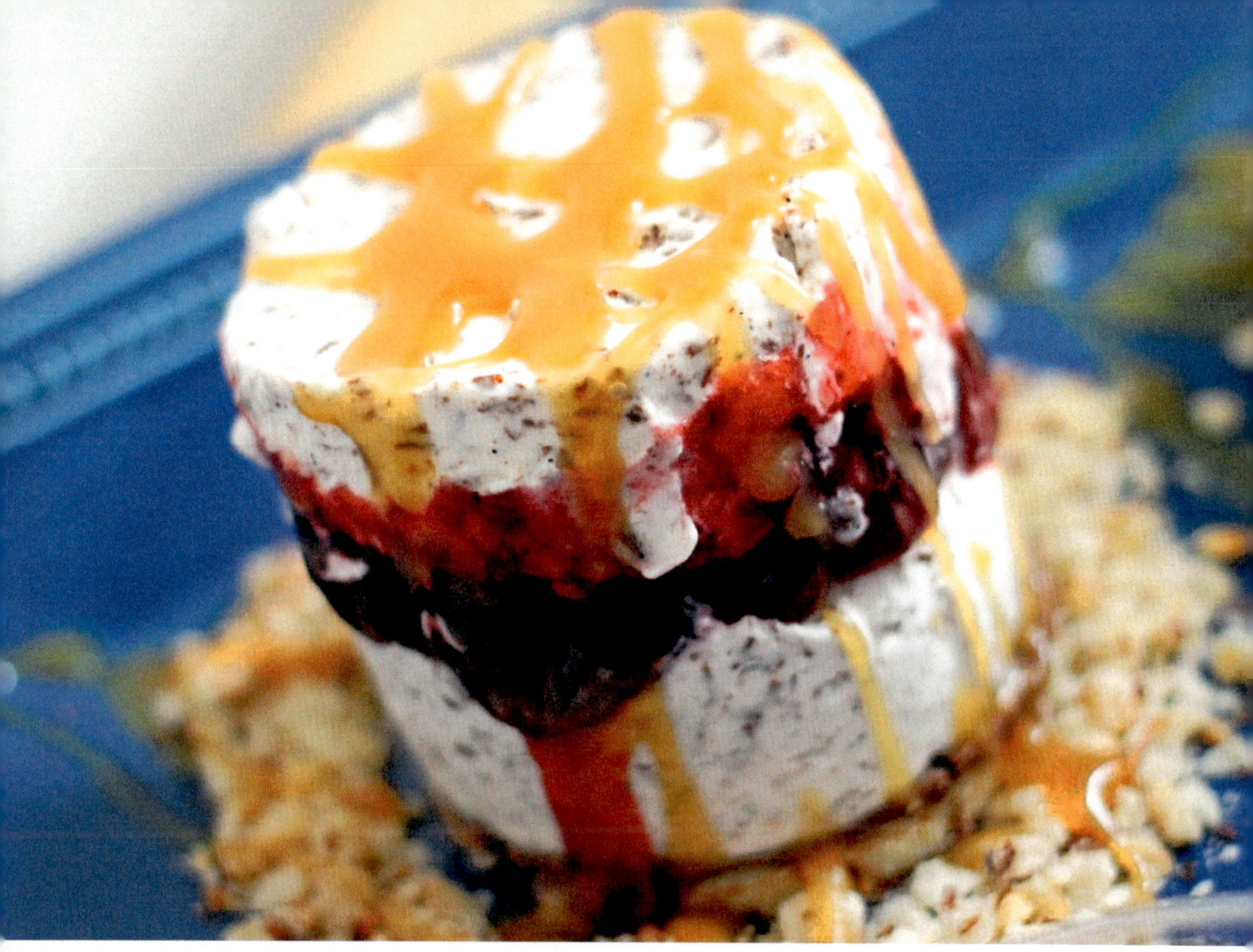
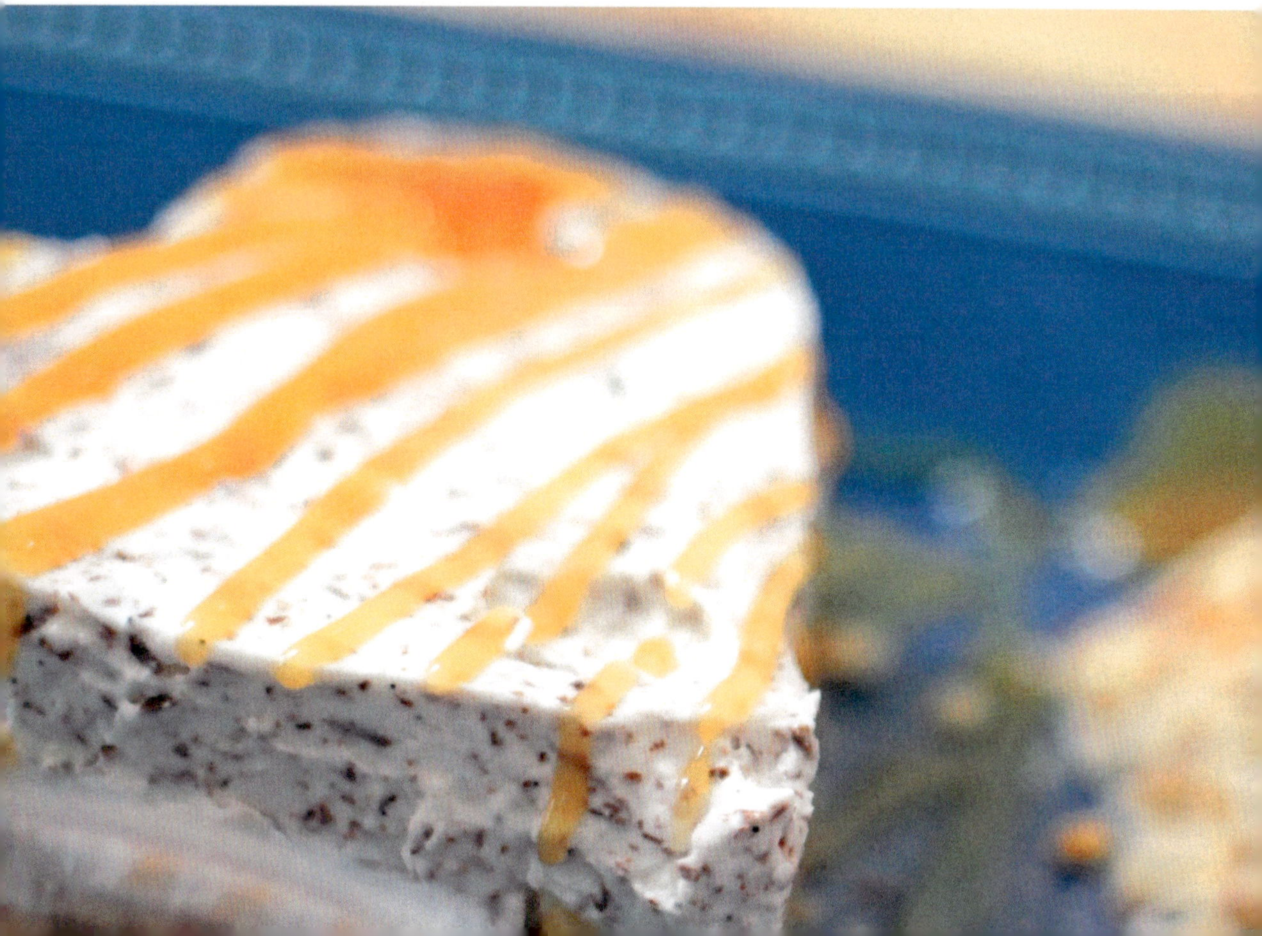

Acknowledgements

Thank you, Velvet Morning Press, for adding this cookbook to your catalogue.

Thank you all for making *Chef Q in Paris: The Fall Collection* successful, and I hope you will enjoy the winter collection as well.

As always, *merci* to my wife for being patient and putting up with my music selection when I'm cooking. I know we don't necessarily share the same musical tastes, but once food is served, all is forgiven, right?!

And last, thank you to my daughter for volunteering to whisk and stir, which inevitably means spending an extra hour in the kitchen. Love you, little chef!

About the Author

Didier, author of *Chef Q in Paris: The Fall Collection* and *Chef Q in Paris: The Winter Collection*, discovered his love of cooking as a seven-year-old growing up in the French countryside. With his grandmother, Didier chose juicy tomatoes, flavorful green beans and delicate herbs from their garden to prepare traditional, seasonal French dishes.

Today, Didier, as "Chef Q Paris," offers private chef services to tourists and locals in Paris, and teaches at The Michel Roux Jr. Cookery School in London. Didier has been cited in articles by Quartz and Bloomberg News, has been a guest on France 24 International News and took part in a pastry documentary with Chef Michel Roux Jr. for the BBC Four as well as "Kitchen Impossible" on U.K. Channel 4.

Didier lives in Paris with his wife and daughter. He is a regular at the local markets and always enjoys a good coffee at his local café.

If you enjoyed these recipes, please leave a review on Amazon! Reviews help other people discover the book, which means you could be helping someone else put a tasty French-inspired meal on their table. *Merci!*

Get *Can You Spell Fromage?* for free (normally $2.99) when you sign up for Didier's mailing list: http://bit.ly/chefq-news

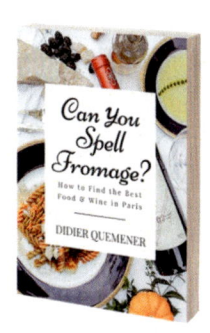

Other Titles

Didier, whose other passion is literature, has contributed short stories to the following collections:

Chef Q in Paris: The Fall Collection
Didier shares his favorite fall recipes and anecdotes in this delicious collection with French flair.

That's Paris: An Anthology of Life, Love & Sarcasm in the City of Light
Escape to Paris through this collection of short stories set in France's famed capital.

Legacy: An Anthology
Stories by best-selling and award-winning authors cover themes of love, friendship and memories in this compelling compilation.

Christmas, Actually
A holiday collection with Christmas spirit, humor and a dash of romance.

Made in the USA
Middletown, DE
17 November 2016